CYCLES IN CYCLES

CYCLES IN CYCLES

BRYAN JOHN FARRELL

ARPress

ILLUMINATING IDEAS.
EMPOWERING VOICES

ARPress
45 Dan Road Suite 5
Canton MA 02021

Hotline: 1(888) 821-0229
Fax: 1(508) 545-7580

Ordering Information:
Quantity sales. Special discounts are available on quantity purchases by corporations, associations, and others. For details, contact the publisher at the address above.

Printed in the United States of America.

| ISBN-13: | Softcover | 979-8-89389-115-7 |
| | eBook | 979-8-89389-114-0 |

Library of Congress Control Number: 2024909035

Table of Contents

Dedicated

to those who believe it is all a big accident,
to those who believe it is a designed plan,
and to those of us just along for the ride.

Characters

John Farrell

Bryan Farrell

Olivera Afua Gilman.

Mary Kelly

Theodore Washington Jones

TW Jones

Lieutenant Ludwick

Boss Sergeant

Azriell Thomas Lynch

Tommy

Introduction

MAYBE FICTION, MAYBE NOT

Can't win with a losing hand, but I keep trying.

As you scrutinize, read and I hope enjoy my nonsense you might think I've spent a lot of time in bars—loser bars to be specific—and you're right and you might wonder why, am I a loser or do I just like to observe losers, and you're right in both scenarios. Be that as it may, I thank God for loser bars. As a matter of fact, I was just in one before writing this introduction. The bar was in the Sierras with a back porch and a grand view of mother nature's artwork. This artwork was not achieved overnight, more like a few hundred million years, years for the tectonic forces to do their thing, drive the Pacific plate over the American plate to a height of over seven thousand feet. Nature doing her thing, eroding out the gorges, steep valleys, planting a carpet of green pine trees, oaks, cottonwood, willows and all just for me to observe after a refreshing vodka tonic. With a back drop noise of people, some too much to drink, telling their stories, I observed a pack of birds in the distance, most likely vultures but I'd like to think eagles, riding almost free on updrafts, effortless gliding above the terrain and I think how lucky they were, I, too, want to glide above the terrain, be able to see in to the folds of earth, peaks, valleys, planes but the best I could do was sip my drink and imagine.

What if you could, but if you can, be careful.

Have you ever had the feeling or maybe a desire that if you turned the next corner, you would be in a different time, a different place with yesteryear's people, smells, and all? I have, possibly unfortunately for you see—I am a dreamer. Often in that space between day and night, a wonderful period of uncertainty, I might be in an older neighborhood, or on an old, abandoned dirt road and there's a turn in the road or a corner in the street that seems out of place, not belonging there. I imagine another world, or a past world, existing just beyond my field of view. I must confess that I'm not sure if what I write about is only fiction or perhaps a bit of truth. You can decide.

Got no choice, hanging on the best you can.

One day, usually after 40, you begin wishing time would slow down. Gone are the days you want time to hurry because you hope you've got better times coming. Now, in an afternoon, enjoying a fine summer afternoon, basking in the warm afterglow of the day, you might want time to slow down and perhaps a song of the past "Stay, stay just a little longer" echoes in your mind.

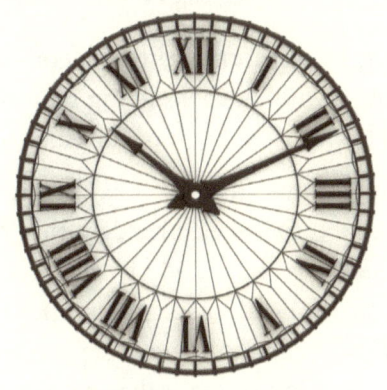

Chapter 1

Life, Time & Energy
Journey of A Want-to-Be Somebody

Caveat first, without any credentials or the where for all to back it up, but here it goes:

Life force, a fundamental element of the universe, pure energy, impervious to time. When the essential ingredients are present, they ignite into life, not necessarily one you recognize.

Time, the fundamental driver of the universe, pure energy (I think), time, life force, and matter are the same, different phases of the same thing.

Photon, pure energy, generated in a Milky Way Star millions of light years away, will experience zero of those light years in its journey to the photon sensitive nerves in your eye. For you see it travels at the same speed as time and therefore no time has passed. To the photon, the journey from the star to the photon sensitive nerves in the back of your eye was instantaneous. But Earth has experienced all that time, millions of years and I have experienced some of that time, time a necessary ingredient of life, of music, of love and for everything precious.

Reflection, sometimes when looking in a mirror, besides noting how age is overtaking my youth, I focus on the pupil, the black hole in the center of the eye and a sense of infinite, endless space, and endless time

1

overwhelms me. I imagine connecting through eons of time to my ancient ancestors, not just human but all those living reproducing organisms, be it fungus or what all, back to the birth of the earth and beyond.

Then I think about how magical it is that reflected light passing through the pupil is converted to electric data that my brain converts to my reality, the scene before me. I am odd by the process and wonder how organic material can be arranged in such a manner to perform that task. Then I reason, I'm a descendent of a line of reproducing living organisms extending back to the creation of earth that perfected the process.

Here on earth, probably just after the surface cooled, a microbe, a very distant ancestor, harvesting mineral of the earth started its life cycle and reproduced a line of living things in their own life cycle that evolved into countless species, some more complex than others, eventually into my human ancestors, eventually to me. A mega large life cycle that my minuscule life cycle revolves within.

Life Cycle

Speaking about cycles: Cycle, things that go around and end up where they started. You can make one by rotating around a point 360 degrees, beginning to end. The diameter can be in time, and it is a variable and therefore the circumference, duration in time, varies, but they all have a beginning and an end. Another way to describe a cycle is a wave function that is interrupted every 360 degrees. Then there are life cycles; we know for sure that people and every other thing have life cycles. Our solar system, the sun and a few other rocky planets, including the rocky planet we call home, have a life cycle.

They say the earth is about 4.5 billion years old and it might be in its third life cycle, the first two ending in a collapse and a rather big explosion. And the earth is in the middle of the third cycle. People who study those things speculate that the universe also has a life cycle, and it's in that life cycle about 15 billion years. Some flies have a life cycle of less than 24 hours. So, all those life cycles, cycles within life cycles. Some life cycles are so small you need a powerful microscope, a high-speed camera to observe it and some are so large you need a powerful telescope, a time-lapse camera to observe it and you need a big imagination in either case.

My life cycle, rather short, is in the earth's life cycle, which is in our solar system's life cycle, which is in our universe's life cycle and who knows what other life cycles the universe is in. Wow, that's a lot of cycles and I wonder if these cycles have the same point they revolve about, concentric, or do they all have their own nonconcentric center point on 3D planes and perhaps entangle periodically? All life cycles involve time and I wonder if they are in the same time domain or are there many time domains. Well, this stuff boggles my mind. Perhaps people in the past condensed all this to simplify into a religion, as the Buddhists samsara, liberation from the cycle of death and rebirth known as reincarnation.

Okay, I will get off my bandwagon but the cycles in cycles stuff Lieutenant Ludwick told me more than a half century ago continues to resonate in my mind. Oh, but you don't yet know about him, you just have to read on if you want to know.

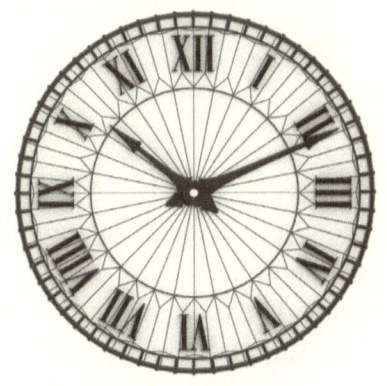

Chapter 2

444 Sussex Street

A Cabin's Life Cycle

Buildings have life cycles, a beginning, and an end, often a brutal end, but it existed for a period, had a function, a purpose.

The Crystal Palace Market, 1175 Market Street, built on a site that once housed a baseball stadium, was a popular San Francisco market, had a three-decade life cycle but ended abruptly, replaced with a hotel.

A Miner's Cabin

Once on a hillside above a canyon, there existed a miner's cabin. It is a long story, but I will try my best to relate it without terribly boring you. Sometimes, the details are necessary to create the suitable scene or maybe it is necessary because I want to give them. The cabin's life cycle commingled with five other life cycles: a slave girl, a slave pirate, an educated negro farmer, a union officer, and a want-to-be someone.

Anyway, the cabin was on the western edge of the old Rancho San Miguel, four thousand odd acres. An 1845 Mexican land grant, granted in the waning days of Mexico rule of Alta California, to Jose de Jesus Noe. John Meirs Horner purchased most of Rancho San Miguel in

1854. Somehow, Alfred Pioche Louis acquired the title, but lost it in a foreclosure sale in 1878.

Theadore Washington Jones, an educated negro farmer then going by TW Jones, bought a large section of the land from the foreclosure. TW Jones divided it into numbered sections suited for resale. The Glen Canyon area, due to the terrain, not really suited for home development, was leased to a cow hollow dairy, The Good Brothers Dairy. TW Jones sold off plots of land to various developers. An acre or so with the abandoned mine and cabin were sold to a female clerk who worked at the local hardware store.

The mine was part of a scam propagated during the 1870s. The scam was generated by some not so honest but ambitious San Francisco businessmen, including two no-count confederate deserters, ex slave pirates, taking advantage of the gold rush fever sweeping America.

The scam. A fraud involved a hole in the ground salted with Sierra Nevada gold, a cabin in the remote San Francisco hills, now called Gold Hill, and a bunch of worthless stock certificates to be sold to Easterners.

The businessmen had long ago departed, but in the 1900s, a barely visible collapsed mine shaft bore witness to the scheme. The Cabin, originally built by those two confederate deserters, want-to-be prospectors, over the years became a house with an address, 444 Sussex Street, San Francisco, California, No Zip Code. In those days, there were no zip codes. You cannot find it today even with a zip code, for it is long gone, but once, it housed a family of Montana refugees.

As a boy, back in the 40s, traces of the mine could still be seen a hundred yards more or less northwest of the house. Sussex Street is a rather long street that runs, mostly level, as it negotiates the terrain of the San Francisco hills. Its pavement ended at Elk Street, a steep, black top over a red brick paved road bordering Glen Canyon. Here, Sussex Street made a hard 280-degree right-hand turn and became a dirt road, weather worn and rutted, a survivor of the past. A hundred or so yards uphill, the road passed the modified cabin, 444 Sussex Street. The first time I remember it being called a miner's cabin was shortly after the Farrell family's migration from the wartime housing projects, an old woman in a handsome, large black shiny auto stopped and through a rolled-down window asked if I was part of the family that just moved into the miner's cabin, and after a long moment, looking at me, she said yes you are one of the special people.

As an unnamed road, the road continued winding its way through a 1000 plus acres of undeveloped remains of the once Rancho San Miguel. Beyond the pavement, there's a feeling you're entering the past, the San Francisco of the 1800s where red tail hawks, ground squirrels, and acres of wild oats existed, undisturbed just as it had for centuries. After the cabin, you entered the realm of the old Rancho San Miguel, untamed. After a few twists and turns, the road narrows along the canyon's edge. Overlooking the canyon was an old campsite, once used by the Ohlone people, seemed to be almost timeless.

In the evening, it was a special, almost magical place. The ocean fog, driven by an eastward breeze, would drift over Mount Davison, forming a fog blanket that cascaded down into the canyon. The sun's rays reflecting off the fog-blanket would cast a reddish orange glow that illuminated the hillside. The breeze and eucalyptus trees would sing softly, a melody you cannot recall, but you seemed to have always known. It was a wonderful place and when day gave away to night, the gateway to the unknown.

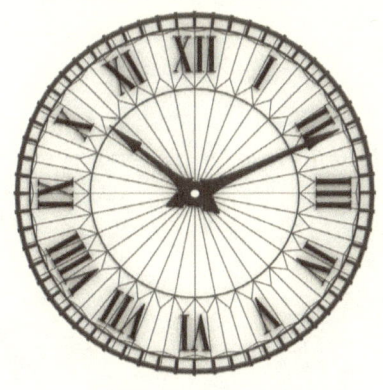

Chapter 3

Farrell Family

California Immigration, The Promised Land

Immigration

The immigration included traveling up the dirt section of Sussex Street, rutted and steep. One had to negotiate the ruts created by years of rainwater draining down from Gold Hill. For countless years, people, horses, mules and what all had labored up and down the road navigating the ruts, in the winter filled with rainwater, and in the summer obscured by dust filled clouds. Only the bravest, horseless carriages would challenge this road. This road was not for the faint of heart but not an issue for an Irish Catholic family, refugees from the high plains of Montana.

The Sussex Street cabin had had multiple owners and many changes over the years and by WW2 had become a multi-room dwelling, a house. It was not a castle, but it was far from the intense high plains heat of a Montana summer and Montana winter's freezing Bitterroot Mountain winds. It was a haven for a dirt farmer's family, a sanctuary from wartime government housing projects, a home, at last, for a large family, a family of six boys and two girls.

The Family 1942

Farrell Family Tale

Before I can move on, I need to describe the events that brought the Montana refugees to San Francisco. I will start with a Stage Stop on the Benton Road or as we knew it, the Mullan Road. The road had been a military project connecting Great Falls, the last navigational port on the Missouri River, to the Pacific Ocean. The road was constructed while the state was still a territory and turned out not to be much of a military asset but found use as a stage road. After the building of the Northern Pacific Railroad, about 1883, the stage route was abandoned, but not the Stage Stop.

Montana State Highway Sign 200

Bird Tail Rock was one of the most prominent landmarks along the Benton Road between Fort Benton and Helena. An igneous intrusion about 55 million years old, it acquired its name because it resembled a 'bird's tail erect and spread out in a fan-shape.' Following an old Indian trail, Lieutenant John Mullan built a road past this extraordinary geological feature in July 1860. The road was on a steep divide about midway between the Sun River and Dearborn River crossings. At first, Mullan was not sure wagons could traverse the rugged terrain here. But after pulling a two-wheel cart over the divide in 1859, his assistant, P.M. Engel, determined the route "practicable for wagons in its present state." With the discovery of gold in southwestern Montana in the early 1860s, the road, now known as Benton Road, was heavily used by freighters and stagecoaches traveling between Fort Benton and Helena. In 1881, a traveler on the road reported that Bird Tail Divide "was more or less dangerous ... and perhaps the most trying piece of stage road in northwestern Montana during the winter season, as the snowdrifts frequently obliterate all traces of (it) for miles."

Old Eagle Rock Station.

Bird Tail Rock Ranch

Once the Eagle Rock Stage Stop, Now A home

JJ Farrell, a teamster, used the Mullan Road to haul freight from Fort Benton to Helena. A good teamster could drive a fully loaded wagon twenty miles in a twelve-hour day. That is on a good day, fair roads, and no major water crossings. But JJ was hauling goods through a couple of hundred miles of improved Indian trails, still claimed by the Black Feet, crossing formidable creeks, sleeping in the open country, caring for himself and his animals. It took weeks of traveling alone, in summer and winter. There would be days when only a few miles were covered.

JJ, a resourceful man, was up to the task. A rancher at heart, he acquired a thousand acres and the abandoned Stage Stop, and named it the Bird Tail Ranch.

St. Peters Mission 1898

It just so happened that the mission of St. Peters was near the stage stop and Lavinia Whitfield was a lay art teacher there.

James J. Farrell, a well-known ranchman on the Muddy, and Miss Lizzie Whitfield of the Mission, were united in marriage at the Catholic church that morning by Father Dols. A few friends of the contracting parties were present. Miss Hanly was the bridesmaid and John Burke the best man. After the ceremony, the happy couple and their friends repaired to the Um house where they partook of an elegant wedding breakfast. [p. 41 (Great Falls Leader Daily 26 Sep 1892]

No one knows how they met, but JJ had a ranch, a wife, and began raising horses and children.

The children, two boys, John and Richard, and a girl, Mary. The two boys lived a long life, but the little girl and her mother succumbed to pneumonia. So, JJ was a bachelor again, but he prospered, selling horses to the US Cavalry at the nearby Fort Shaw, and busy raising the boys. The boys inherited the Bird Tail Rock ranch when JJ succumbed to the 1918 influenza epidemic. The boys married and they and their wives shared the Stage Stop for a few years, but John, in a dispute with a neighbor, some say over his wife, killed the neighbor. The legal cost to defend John and the downturn in livestock profits resulted in the ranch's foreclosure by the Land Bank of Montana.

Backup plan The Homestead

It's said being poor is a state of mind. Sometimes, it's a reality, so Richard and wife Marion homesteaded 80 acres on the Bench some 50 odd miles from Great Falls. They and their four children moved there and started wheat farming. John mysteriously acquired a few hundred debt free acres in Western Montana and continued in the livestock business.

Homestead painted by Marion Farrell 1968

So, with 80 irrigated acres, 6000ft elevation, in the harsh unpredictable Montana environment, it is difficult to make a living. Through twelve lean depression years they scraped out a living but now with seven mouths to feed, three additional born on the homestead, Richard and Marion found it difficult to make ends meet. Then Johnny, the baby of the family, possibly a mistake, after all Mrs. Farrell had seven bright, intelligent, handsome children, she did not need one more, but maybe she thought he would be the best and what the hell, he was only one more to raise and make an even eight. It turns out he was a bigger problem than she bargained for, a rebel without a clue, a dreamer, but that's another story. Fortunately for the Farrell clan, Europe exploded into a battleground. WW2 started, and the demand for labor provided the clan a needed exodus. They set off for San Francisco; the shipyard was hiring, in a 36 Chevy, a terrier mutt dog, a basket of fried chicken, a couple of hundred dollars and eight kids.

Eight Kids and Courage

Marion, the matriarch of the Farrell brood, claimed she had two families, four children born at the Bird Tail Ranch and four born at the Homestead. So, in hopes I do not bore you as I do my family due diligence, I will proceed with a description of the Farrell progenies.

Four Ranch Kids

Not claiming to be creative, I'll just start with the first, oldest child, Richard Henry jr., born in the spring of '21, along with calves, lambs, and poults. That's 1921 on the JJ Farrell's Ranch, the Bird Tail Ranch. Richard Henry jr. was a full-term offspring, not always the case with newlyweds. He was a beautiful baby boy, with blond hair, blue eyes, and a loving disposition. But 444 Sussex was never his home, being in his early twenties and old enough to be on his own, he never lived there.

Gwendolyn, a Christmas gift of 1922, was always just Gwen, the second child, my oldest sister. For Gwen, 444 Sussex Street was a way station, a place awaiting the return of her reluctant WW2 warrior Jimmy, a second lieutenant artillery officer in the army and deployed in the Pacific Campaign. They had been friends, or maybe young lovers, before the war. Gwen was strikingly attractive with many potential suitors, but Jim was her true love.

He had joined the ROTC, a product of WW1, to help subsidize college fees. He was part of the young avant-garde of Montana's Carroll College. A rural renaissance man, Jim was an artist at heart, not a worrier. He was commissioned a First Lieutenant in 1939, just in time for the big show and fought in several major Pacific battles, including Guadalcanal, Okinawa, Philippines.

I asked him many years later how he had survived the war, and he said, "The first thing I did was to dig a hole and keep my head down". He went on to say he only lost one soldier and that was because he did not dig a hole and keep his head down.

Gordon, the undisputed genius of the family, was hardheaded and too smart for his own good. Born on April 18 but 15 years earlier than Johnny. One story has it that an argument got so hot during a return from church that the family had to kick him out of the car and made him walk the last ten miles to the homestead. High school graduate at 14, college graduate at 16 and medical school graduate at 22. He was a medical doctor at 22, but in the long run could not accept being just a mortal and passed away at 52.

Harvey was more of a free spirit and a lover. He was the tallest of the boys and set on living as soon as possible. 444 Sussex, for him, was only temporary. He quit school and started working as an auto mechanic, fell in love with a beautiful redheaded young lady, moved out and did whatever was necessary to keep her happy.

Four Homestead Children

I'm going to continue the Farrell family story about the four homestead kids. Charles, usually Chuck, born December 3, 1933, in the Great Depression. The first child conceived on the 80-acre homestead was the best looking of the boys, at least he thought so and I agree, but then all the Farrell boys were good looking. Chuck was studious and committed to improving his lot, for you see many of our neighbors looked down on us—that large family living in that upgraded cabin.

"You know, they raise chickens there and eat them, fried chicken, for Sunday dinner."

Well, Chuck succeeded in self-supporting for four years at UC Berkeley, an engineering degree, and a job in the southern California Aerospace Industry.

Janette Denise, a Christmas gift of 1935, was the youngest daughter. To her, 444 Sussex Street was her first taste of luxury. Within a few years, Gwen departed with her lover Jim, and Janette had her own bedroom. It was on the third floor that was originally part of the attic. She was the only one with a room to herself. The three boys had to share rooms, but then we had low expectations and were happy to have a roof over our heads. She was rather an attractive young lady who managed her young life well. It might have been perfect except for her younger brat brother, Johnny, whom she loved to beat up just for entertainment.

No, we were not *The Brady Bunch,* we were more the typical family with lots of sibling rivalry. She did well in school and with the goal of a better education, she attended a highly regarded Catholic High School. She was popular there and was voted senior school president. Her future looked bright, and she headed to college, but college did not suit her fancy and she shortly switched to a downtown paying job. She had several suitors, and she chose a handsome young Hispanic plumber, Joe, to pursue her new career as a housewife. Their future looked promising: kids, a house in the suburbs, a new Buick, and so on. But Joe had roving eyes and one thing led to another and when Janette had had enough, they divorced.

Michael, born just after New Year 1938, another handsome, intelligent boy, the matriarch should have stopped there, but no and so, he was Johnny's older brother, had to look out for his nitwit younger brother. Thank God.

Bryan John, the last to be conceived on the homestead, the want-to-be somebody. Hell, you are going to know too much about him since he's writing this nonsense.

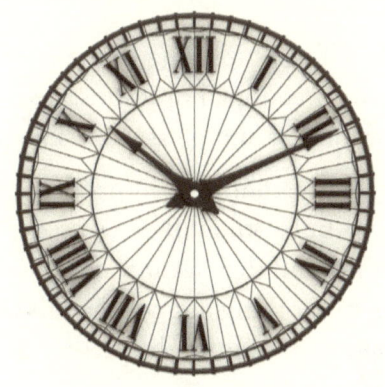

Chapter 4

The Sixth Son

Six Sons, Seventh Son's Luck Saga of Johnny

L ive in the moment, the mantra of the 'free love' generation, the grandchildren of the 'lost' generation, was live in the moment. That's not my generation. Johnny's generation was the 'no name' generation (NNG). A generation, somewhere between the 'lost' and 'free love' generation. You may not have heard of the NNG, the children of the Depression. And you might think I am making them up, just a literary ploy, but they existed, just not as boisterous as those other generations. And so, I have to say the NNG is a generalization of a small partition of Johnny's generation, Johnny and a few other San Francisco kids with an attitude. They had no big ideology, just took what's given and dealt with it. Be that as it may, I've tried to understand what those words, lost, free, love, and moment mean and what they describe about each generation. Here are some definitions:

> Lost: "unable to find one's way; not knowing one's whereabouts."
>
> Free: "not or no longer confined or imprisoned."
>
> Love: "a great interest and pleasure in something."
>
> Moment: "a very brief period of time."

So, then I wonder: If you are living in the moment for "a very brief period of time" "no longer confined or imprisoned," "not knowing one's whereabouts," "a great interest and pleasure in something?"

Okay they were clearly confused, impatient, clueless but I am also confused and impatient but I know they wanted sex, no responsibility, did not want to pay for it and they want it now, in the present. But hell, we all want something for nothing but we, the NNG, were willing to pay but did not know where to find it, in the present or the past.

Past or present: It takes about 1/50th of a second for a scene before you to convert (reflected light your eyes receive via electrical signals to the brain) to the images you see. Accordingly, your perception of the present is 1/50th of a second in the past. Therefore, I had a difficult time understanding exactly what the present is? A definition: the period of time now occurring. But actually, the vision, the scene before me now, the scene I perceive as the present, the period of time now occurring, my reality is actually in the past.

So, I think the best, the closest to the present I can get is 20 milliseconds in the past. I would like to live in the moment, but how can I, if my perception of the present is always in the past? I keep looking for the answer, but now I am not sure I know the question, not sure if it's about the present or the past. My point is that separating the past from the present is not always clear. So, I'll try not to belabor this stuff, but as my life cycle is at point A, my perception, my reality of the present, is at point B, in the past. Every item seen or heard is in the past. What's unknown is what happens between point A and point B, that period of unknown, concealed to the conscious mind. 20 milliseconds might seem insignificant in our life cycle, but that photon has traveled six million meters in its life cycle. Okay, I don't have a clue about this whole thing, past, present, or life cycles, but consider this: From the photon perspective, a person's life cycle would look like a pixel on a huge TV screen, finitely small insignificant dots, but the life cycle of the photon from a person's perspective is infinitely large, incomprehensible, immense like the night sky's Milky Way.

Johnny's Bedroom

I am going to change the subject to try to keep it interesting. Johnny's bedroom was in a converted attic in the cabin with a single small window. It was cozy and warm, despite the bare wood infrastructure and cedar roof shingles, with daylight shining through, but waterproof, never leaked, not even in the biggest rainstorms. While the single small window provided little light, it provided plenty of fresh air; you see, it would not quite shut. Besides fresh air, it allowed the night's song generated by the ever-present westward wind and the old big blue gum eucalyptus just outside the window. The Farrells tried to eliminate it by cutting it down, but the blue gum eucalyptus just regrew, bigger than ever. He shared the room and bed with his older brother, Mike, until Harvey, one of the older brothers, left for L.A. in pursuit of his lady friend. Mike then moved into the larger bedroom, which he shared with Chuck. While Johnny's bed was small, it was a step up from the bed in the bottom drawer in an old chest of drawers in the homestead.

Just Tough Enough

Turkeys were domesticated about 2,000 years ago. The bird is a distant relative of the chicken but is much larger, about head high and equal in weight to a three-year-old boy. To subsidize the homestead income, Mrs. Farrell raised turkeys for sale. The income was sorely needed, but this created a big problem for Johnny, getting from the porch to the barn, only about 100 feet, but to Johnny it seemed more like a half a mile. The turkeys were free to roam the yard, and the turkeys preferred to hang out between the porch and the barn. So, every morning there would be a big fight between Johnny and the gobblers. Before he could get to the barn, he had to fight it out with a number of head-high gobblers. He would have one hell of a fight getting into the barn, but it was really important to get there cause Mr. Farrell, his dad, would be milking the cow. Johnny would bring his tin cup for Dad to fill it with warm cow's milk. Have you ever tasted warm cow's milk fresh from the cow? It is unforgettable; you taste so much more than just milk, earth, grass, and cow. Yes, the cow! That is why your milk cows are special, not a run-of-the-mill cow. A cow who produces sweet rich milk with the flavor of the earth. Bottled milk is counterfeit milk. Yes, pasteurized milk is safer, but so is safe sex, but not as good. Well, anyway, and fortunately for little Johnny, this fighting stuff would come in handy.

Milk Carton Kid

Johnny might be special to some, but he sure did not think so in the 4th grade. In school, he was known as a Milk Carton Kid, the kid who looked so undernourished, he was taken out of class in the morning for a carton of milk and graham crackers. He was dyslexic and a dialectical thinker. He thought and saw differently then other kids and could not read or spell worth a damn. He would be taken out of the classroom for special-ed classes and to top it off, he'd gotten ringworm in his hair. The cure in the day was Mercurochrome, and a shaved head. The Mercurochrome, an organomercurial disodium salt compound, produces purple blotches covering the infected areas. He had to wear a cut off top section of a women's nylon stocking as a hat. He was a small skinny kid, wearing his big brother's clothes, purple spots on his head and women's nylon stockings tied in a knot as a cap. But luckily, he was just smart enough, a bit athletic, the fastest runner, a good kickball player and just tough enough—thanks to the turkey gobblers on the homestead—to be tolerated if not respected by his classmates.

Johnny's Big Accident, 1947

He was seven, and the accident occurred at the intersection of Sussex and Mizpah Streets. A 1947 collision between Johnny on a pilfered bike and a 1938 black Cadillac. He was riding a bicycle on the Sussex Street sidewalk. The bike was stolen, most likely acquired a few nights earlier on his brother's paper route. It was hand painted black by its former owner. Most likely, he'd stolen it too and changed its color. The bike had a defective coaster brake. Sometimes, when you applied the brake, rotating the pedal backwards, the pedal would just rotate freely. The driver of the car was coming up Mizpah Street, a rather steep grade in his 1938 Cadillac, most likely late for something. Johnny tried to brake and stop the bike. Anyway, Johnny got the worst of it. He only remembered the big black hood and then waking up on a nearby neighbor's bed. He got off easy with only a black eye and some bruises, somewhat changed but in the same universe.

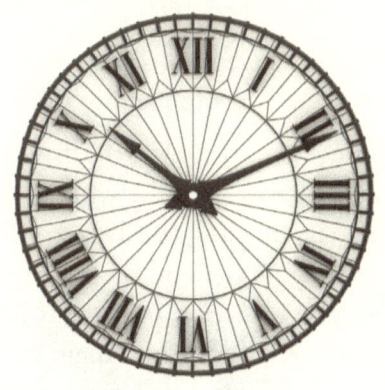

Chapter 5

Olivia Meeting

Gateway to the Unknown

June 20, 1948, San Francisco Campsite

Ohlone people's campsite on the old Rancho San Miguel was precious, special, and Johnny only occasionally visited it. It was unique, and he felt if he overdid it, it would lose its magic. For you see, Johnny was one of those special students, so-called challenged, requiring special ed classes. It was not for lack of smarts. His IQ placed him in the gifted category, but he'd preferred not to deal with the rest of the world. But that's another story.

One evening, after a rather difficult day, being assigned to the retarded row in Mrs. Johnson's 5th grade class, (a row of five or six seats against the wall that was assigned to sub-performing, difficult students) he sought the solace of the site. The retarded-row assignment was not a big deal. He knew he was smart enough. It was that new student directly behind him that did not understand "back-off". He continued his constantly annoying activities. Johnny retaliated with a warning punch, which knocked him to the floor. Johnny did not think he punched that hard, but Mrs. Johnson retaliated by sending Johnny to the principal's—

Mrs. Terwilliger—office for a lecture—"Why can't you be good like the rest of the Farrell kids?"—on behaving and to be sent home.

Anyway, that evening Johnny visited the campsite. A refuge, a place just for himself. He built a small campfire with dry eucalyptus twigs and stayed later than usual. The burning eucalyptus filled the night air with a pleasant aroma. His thoughts were on the events of the day, to tell the truth, I'm not sure if this was a dream but here it is: Johnny had no idea where, how or when she arrived but then there was a young girl sitting across the campfire. It was difficult to tell in the firelight, but she seemed to be young; a rather pleasing looking fair skin negro girl dressed in homespun but nicely tailored old-fashioned clothes. For some reason, he felt quite comfortable with her company.

After a moment of shared appraisal, she said with a southern accent, "Johnny, I am Afua. I did not mean to startle you, but this campfire was so compelling. I have always loved it, for you see, I've been here many times a long time ago. Do you know you are one of the special people? You know the secret."

"What secret?" Johnny asked.

"The time veil, but you must be careful," she replied.

"Careful of what?" Johnny asked.

"Knowledge, it can free you, but then again, it can encumber you. Sometimes, it might be smarter to wear blinders," she replied.

"So, what are you doing here? How did you get here and how did you know my name?" Johnny asked.

"I really do not know, except I've been here many times, when I lived in that miner's cabin, and then you were here. The night is beautiful, and I decided a visit was in order. So would you like it if I told you a story, my story?" she replied.

"Well, I love stories as long as it is not a scary one," replied Johnny.

"Olivia was my slave name, but Afua (Friday's child) from my Ghana roots is my given name."

She continued without waiting for any response, "Asha, my mother, named me Afua. While I'll respond to Olivia, my slave family has always used my African name. I was born April 18, 1847, in Louisiana on a sugar cane plantation somewhere in the Mississippi delta area, exactly where, I don't know. My father, Mr. Gilman, Claire, the plantation mistress' brother, lived in Shreveport. He would occasionally visit his sister on the plantation. In those days, it was a custom for a family member's visit to last for weeks. While these visits would occur on a regular basis, it started occurring more often, and Claire suspected it had something to do with a particular young slave girl. While conception was an accident, the love that produced it was genuine. You see, Mr. Gilman and my mother were in love. History is full of stories of noble men falling in love with women of different classes, barmaids, kitchen servants and why not a beautiful slave girl, you know that has happened many times. William the Conqueror's mother was a bar maiden.

"My father and mother had fallen in love. You know that can happen, even in that situation, the strict southern color code. Typically, it was swept under the rug, but not in this case. Mr. Gilman had planned to move with my mother to California and to face what may come to live free with the woman he loved. But first, he needed to raise money to buy my mother and the fare to San Francisco. But my mother, dear soul, passed away, yellow fever, while I was still suckling. Mr. Gilman was overcome in his grief, drifted off and joined the Union Army, not sure but maybe to eliminate slavery. After the war, he, my father, settled in North Carolina, married a young Catholic girl. You know, that makes us cousins, although long distant cousins, well maybe half cousins. We share European blood, but that's still blood. Seems we have a couple of things in common, blood and that cabin.

"The mistress of the plantation took pity. After all, I was her illegitimate niece and had one of the house negroes, a mid-aged African woman, Hibo, to care for me. Claire, the plantation mistress, was a good Christian woman who accepted that benevolent owner's philosophy that negroes were better off being slaves. She saw nothing wrong with owning slaves. After all, her grandfather had risked everything, including his life, to develop the plantation and slaves were essential. The plantation had been nothing more than mosquito infested swamp land and now it was one of the best plantations in the delta.

"Well, Mrs. Claire Marion Bryant developed a real attachment for me and named me Olivia, after her first cousin on her father's side. She did not want to see me, this beautiful child and her niece turned into a field negro or even a house negro, but she had a dilemma because her husband considered me property worth $400 and he ruled the house. Mrs. Bryant had an older uncle who was a tailor. He was known to be a kind and loving man, not too religious. He had a habit of cursing out the local church leader and most of the convocation, particularly regarding this benevolent trash, he was an abolitionist at heart but thought the northerners had no business telling Southerners what to do, like the English butting into Ireland's business. Mrs. Bryant had a proposition for her uncle, James Kelly. Even though he was Catholic, she felt he would care for Olivia. After all, they are blood related. She would pay my slave fee and he would raise and tutor me in the tailoring craft and, at some point, give me freedom.

That was a good plan, but like most plans, they don't always work, in my case because, in the process of raising and educating me, he learned to love me as a daughter and was reluctant to free me. He feared I would leave, and he would miss me so. Like so many parents, he could not bear the thought of his child moving on, living their own life on their terms. But that is the nature of life. Eventually, the children will or must leave the nest.

"I knew I was pretty, but as I matured into a young woman, I was surprised by the attention I got from men, black and white. I had African blood, would be judged a negro woman, but I knew I also had European blood. While people considered me African, I knew I was born and bred an American. I sought to be a free American woman. I was most grateful to James, my master-father, who treated me as his child with love and respect. I did not like it but understood that in public, he had to tow the slave line for both of our wellbeing, especially with all the uproar caused by northern abolitionists. But except for a brief moment when dealing with customers, I was treated as his lass, a daughter.

"In private, James would call me Sunset because I came to him late in life. I would confide my feelings as a daughter might to a father. But people have feelings and desires they share with no one, sometimes not even their own conscious being, their identity. A young girl's prince charming might be one of these desires she'll not share.

"My prince charming was always a young white man, wealthy, charming, gentle who would sweep me off my feet and away from this dreadful place, slavery, with its deep southern roots and prejudice. There was that young confederate officer, the Lynch Boy, I tailored a uniform for. I could sense his desire and thought he would be back, but I felt he was not my prince. But I could not get that beautiful, handsome black man, Theodore Washington Jones, the man I was also tailoring a suit for, out of my mind. He had none of the property I was looking for, but by God, I felt he was one I could spend my life with, come what may.

"Well, Johnny, do you want me to continue my story? You see, I lived for a while in the cabin back in the day, long before it became 444 Sussex, as you know it. There was an incident in Logan's Corner, that's where the tailor shop was located, that nearly cost me my life, but I think I will let Theodore Washington Jones himself tell you, oh that's right, you have not met him yet."

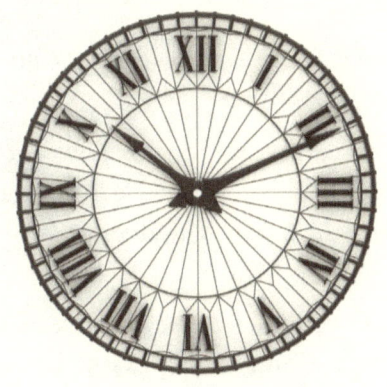

Chapter 6

Becoming Bryan

Johnny becoming Bryan
A Sailor's Odyssey, 1957
A Dirt Bike Rider, 1970

Johnny was a young man, 17, when he joined the Navy and only spent four years of his life cycle as a sailor, but it had a major impact on his life. It was like his baptism into real life. He was Johnny when he enlisted and became Bryan. He'd spent a few weeks in juvenile detention, saw the writing on the wall—change your ways, young man. The Navy gave him the opportunity. But initially, the Navy was not sure they wanted this boy with a broken nose and a jailhouse stare.

The first thing the Chief Petty officer in charge of the new recruits said was, "Farrell, you'll never make it. I've seen your kind before."

No Options, Not Going Back

And Johnny becoming Bryan thought, *Hell I must make it because the alternative is to be a failure and I will prove to you and the world I am not a failure. If I can't make it through Navy Boot Camp like millions of men have, I will be a nobody, a real loser.*

Well, the Chief did everything in his power to make his prophecy come true; ostracized, extra bathroom cleaning duty, midnight watch every night, but Bryan said to himself, *You can kill me but you cannot get me to quit.*

The Chief, in desperation, sent Bryan to a Navy psychologist who interrogated him and gave him an IQ exam. Bryan did not know the results, but things changed. It seemed the Chief could now tolerate him, if not appreciate him. But Johnny, now Bryan, learned he could handle whatever came his way, a discipline that has served him well.

USS *Bennington*

Upon completing bootcamp, Bryan, okay, I received orders to report to The USS Bennington in the San Francisco shipyards. The USS Bennington was a WW2 Essex Class Carrier updated for jet fighters, Korea era fighters like the North American FJ-3 Fury, and Grumman F9F/F-9 Cougar, not really first line fighters. She was basically an outdated, jinxed, and expendable aircraft carrier, 14 years into her 50 year life cycle. Word on the ship was that she had been transferred from the Atlantic to the Pacific fleet to keep a crew. Sailors would transfer if they could; they did not want to serve on her. She'd had two major explosions in the near past—catapult and boiler—that killed a number of sailors.

One explosion, not really an explosion, was more of an accident. The downcomer, a two-feet-in-diameter pipe containing super-heated steam, broke loose and filled the fire room with super-heated steam. The boiler accident was in the number one fire room, the one I was assigned to. The Essex Class Carrier had four fire rooms, two boilers, manufactured by Babcock and Wilcox, per fire room. Each fire room had a crew of 35 or so personnel assigned to it. During the turn-to-hours, 0800–1600, most of the 35 crew would be in their respective fire rooms. There were three watches, eight hours each, and they were rotated to even the load. The accident killed the whole Graveyard Watch, 0000–0400 hours, which had only shortly since taken the watch.

While the ship is in port and docked, the boilers are shut down and offline, cold iron. The fire room would be quiet, and sailors would say they could hear the dead crew walking about during the Graveyard Watch. After the boilers were restarted and the fire room warmed, the metal would expand, and it seemed like you could smell the flesh of the doomed third watch crew. Anyway, those accidents were a few years in the past and Bennington was my new home for a while in the San Francisco shipyard. So, what does a sailor do on liberty in his hometown? Hookup with an old girlfriend, of course. Well, push came to shove and I, Bryan, was a married man at seventeen.

The Home Port for the Bennington was San Diego, and after some repairs, the ship departed San Francisco to her home port. So, I'm in San Diego and my new wife is in San Francisco. What a mess, very little money and 600 miles from my main squeeze.

Hitchhiking, Wheel of Fortune

I'd often hitchhike some 1200 odd miles from San Diego, my ship's home base, to San Francisco and back on a 72-hour liberty pass. To tell the truth, I enjoyed the adventure. Oh, and it was an adventure. I would meet mostly outstanding people, but now and then some weirdos. What I found was that people who stopped and gave me a ride were above average people. A lot of WW2 vets who knew the deal, some truck drivers needing company, a few high-level executives just because, and of course, gay men wanting to hit on me. But hitting on me was the exception; mostly, the rides were more of a gift with no strings attached.

August 1958, Deployment

Meet Lieutenant Ludwick, Storyteller or Coincidence

A ride to remember. First, the caveat, it's been many years and sometimes, I'm not sure if it's one of those dreams hard to discern from reality. For sure, the ride, the T Bird, was real but the Lieutenant, unsure.

But here it goes: It was about 0500 (5 a.m.), I was on my return trip back to San Diego. My ship, the USS Bennington CVA 20, named for a 1777 battle, would deploy for the Far East at 0700 hours (7 a.m.).

I had no clue why the ship was ordered for this deployment; it was not routine because we had just finished sea trials, a major upgrade in the San Francisco shipyard. I thought the ship would hang around the Pacific coast for a few months, but this was not the case. Unscheduled deployment.

Sorely Needed Ride

Okay, back to the ride story. I was somewhere in Los Angeles; it was getting late; the ship departed at 0700 and I was worried about missing the ship's departure. To miss deployment was a big deal, severely punished. It was early morning, about 0500 hours, and I was looking at a two-and-a-half-hour trip, the drive, catch the ferry and so-on. Hitchhiking on the freeways was risky. The police or the shore patrol would pick you up, but the freeway was the only feasible solution to my dilemma. So, to quote Admiral Farragut, "Damn the torpedoes, full steam ahead," and to the Los Angeles freeways I went in search of the badly needed ride.

That early in the morning, there's very little traffic and none on the freeway-on-ramp, so I had to move on to the freeway proper. On the freeway, Highway 101 then, now Interstate 5, a Red 56 T Bird was pulled over to the side of the freeway and a bearded man with straggly long hair dressed in a civil war uniform, hat, boots and all, was standing next to it.

I thought, *Maybe he is heading home from a late-night costume party and had a car problem or something; or maybe he's just three sheets to the wind and needs a driver; be careful.* But I was a desperate sailor, so I approached him and asked him if he needed any help.

He looked at me, eyes clear, steady, he was not intoxicated; he replied with a soft southern accent, "I am Lieutenant Ludwick, I'm going to Mexico."

I thought, *Okay, he wants to keep up the charade and I can live with that if I can get the ride I need.*

I volunteered, "Maybe I should drive; I was going in that direction."

So, to make a long story short and it has been many years, and I am not, or perhaps not sure I want to be, sure of the details, but he agreed and in his soft southern accent, I thought he said, "You're running late so we best be getting on with it."

Now, how in the hell could he know? Is he also a fortune teller or something? Okay, I figured he must be ex-navy and now thinks he is a Army lieutenant or something, but he guessed correctly about my situation.

Without looking at me, he continued, "You know, we have something in common. We both lived in a cabin TW Jones owned."

I thought, *Who in the hell is this TW Jones? I don't know any TW Jones. If I wasn't so desperate for this ride, I could forget the whole thing, just turn, and head down the road and try to catch another ride, but I'll play along, because I need this ride.*

But I said, "Who's TW Jones? And what cabin?"

When he replied, "The educated Negro Farmer, that cabin on gold hill, the one next to the sham gold mine."

I became concerned and thought *this must be a joke or something. How can this be?* Damn if I didn't need this, but I do, so I said, "Okay, whatever."

Back in the day, 1954 to be specific, Ford Motor Company decided that they needed a car to compete with General Motors' Corvette and the car was the Thunderbird, not the two-headed bird but a quasi-sport car. So, with the help of a former GM executive and some talented craftsmen, a clay model of their creation was shown at the 1954 Auto Show and in 1956, a metal version went on sale. It was a two-seat car modeled after the Jaguar XK120 with Ford Y-Block 312 cubic inch V8 engine and a 3-speed automatic.

So off we went, me driving and him sitting quietly, calmly as a passenger. Have you ever heard a Y-Block 312 cubic inch V8 engine with a 3-speed automatic wide open, it lopes in a methodical rhythm.

I had two hours for a two-and-a-half-hour trip.

In those days, the freeway only extended part way to San Diego, a good deal was still on the old Pacific Highway, a two-way road. Well, I drove that T bird as fast as I thought I could get away with, fully expecting to be pulled over by the CHP or some other local police or a request from the passenger to slow down, but I felt like do-or-die.

A few minutes after pulling onto the freeway, he started to tell me a story about a Civil War Battle. He asked, "Have you ever heard about the Very Little Battle at Logan's Crossroads?"

And without waiting for a reply launched into a nearly 100-year-old tale. "You will not find it in the history books because I made up the name to describe an event that occurred at Logan's Crossroads back in the day. I had sent Theodore to be fitted for a suit. He was a young black man, a neighbor back in Ohio. The local called him the Educated Negro Farmer, because he was quite well educated. You see, that was unusual for the time. He had just escaped the rebels' army, army of Tennessee, and was wearing rags for clothes, wanted to join my outfit to fight the rebels and needed new clothes.

I did not want to interrupt this tale. I was afraid the want-to-be lieutenant might notice how I was driving, but I couldn't help myself and I asked, "How did your neighbor get in the rebel army?"

The want-to-be lieutenant without looking at me said, "Those slave pirates, the Lynch boys, they seized him, claimed he was an escaped slave and were on the way to the slave market when intercepted by a confederate platoon and he and the slave pirates, were forced into the rebel's army, and Theodore became property of the rebel army but that's another story."

Another story, I thought. *Okay, whatever, just keep talking and don't be concerned about my driving.*

And he continued, but I paid little attention. I was too busy driving and watching for cops.

Seemingly unaware my fast aggressive driving, he continued his story "Due to the war, store-bought clothing was not an option, and I understood there was a tailor shop in nearby Logan's Crossroads. I sent a couple of soldiers to safeguard him, he needed protection with all the slave stuff. I do not know the exact details, but here's what my soldiers told me.

"Theodore, after being fitted, was informed by the seamstress, Olivia, that some rebels were going to bushwhack him at the stables; so, one of my troopers circled around the back of the stables. Oh, I should tell you about Olivia, but no. She told you herself, years ago, do you recall? But right now, I want to finish this story."

Olivia told me herself? I don't know any Olivia, I thought, but had an uneasy feeling, a memory of a young girl by a fire pit.

Continuing his story the want-to-be Lieutenant said "Theodore, and the troopers assigned to protect him, left the shop to retrieve their horses at the livery station, just down the road a bit. The soldier pointed at a suspicious-looking wagon across the road; it seemed to be fully loaded with two Tennessee mules still in harness. Men stood up from behind it and one bellowed, 'Put down your arms. You are under arrest and war prisoners of the Army of Tennessee.'

"So, my trooper shouted back, 'Under arrest? What the hell are you jabbering about? Aren't you the Lynch boy? What are you doing in that rebel officer's uniform? I heard you were on your way to California.'

"Then my other escort trooper stepped out from the stable and shouted, 'No, you damn rebels, put down your weapons. You are under arrest by the Army of Mississippi.'

"Then a few frenzied shots were fired. Nobody knows who fired first but then the Tennessee mules jolted and started running, loaded wagon and all, with the young rebels following, running as fast as they could, trying to catch the wagon. My men started laughing as they described the rebels chasing their runaway mules and loaded wagon.

"One of my troopers noticed a man, the old Irishman, kneeling over a body lying in the road. It was Olivia lying in the road, her face covered with blood. She must have been in the wrong place at the wrong time, and the old Irishman, James, thought she was dead. So, Theodore noticed all the commotion, wanders over and checks her pulse. He cleaned her face and said, 'No, she is not dead, just a slight head wound; be just fine in a day or so.'

The want-to-be lieutenant still seemingly unaware of my near reckless driving said "I heard the very next month Olivia was on her way to San Francisco. It seems the old Irishman decided it was time to free her. His brother, Michael, had a dry goods store there and Olivia could work for him. I think that was a good decision because she would have a safe place to live, less prejudice and far from his civil war and hypocrisy."

He paused for a moment, I thought he's going to asked me to slow down but instead he said" Olivia will filling the details"

Wow, about this time I thought: *he may not be intoxicated but he must be plum crazy. What kind of nonsense is this? How in the hell could Olivia tell me her story if she's dead, or 120 or so years old, and in an assisted living facility somewhere, who knows? But the name Olivia stirred something in my memory, a very old memory of a girl by the campfire. But right now, I didn't want to deal with it.*

Okay, I'll go along with whatever, as long as he doesn't mind my driving.

I drove the 120 miles and arrived at the Nickel Snatcher's—the ferry to North Island Navy Base—parking lot just before the ferry left the pier.

Lieutenant Ludwick looked at me and said, "The answer is clear. You can see it in every day and in every venue. Everything is a cycle, cycles in cycles, cycles with minuscule to infinite time periods. You cannot escape your cycle, but occasionally, you might get a glimpse into another."

I was dumbfounded, a two-hour drive, nonsense about a long-forgotten battle and then this cycle stuff. I figured this civil war stuff must be a story his grandfather told him, and maybe his grandfather was a Union Lieutenant, and he was putting me on, acting out the lieutenant part or something but there was no time for philosophy, so I gave him a salute and ran for the ferry. Ran the last mile from the ferry landing to the ship's dock and boarded the USS Bennington CVA 20 just a few minutes before the gangplank was pulled.

In Harm's Way

This deployment was an emergency deployment to the Philippine Sea to head off the Chinese Red Army. Bennington and I were heading for the Formosa Straits to keep a lot of Red Chinese on their side of the straits. We were going to be sitting ducks, between two warring parties, the Chinese PLA, and Taiwan's ROC. After departing San Diego, we picked up an Air Group; I think ATG-4 air task group and special weapons, atomic weapons, at the Alameda Navy Air Station, then proceeded pretty much at flank-speed through a large typhoon directly to the Straits of Taiwan. By the time we reached the straits, the Bennington had outrun its escort warships, assigned to protect her, and she and us were on our own. Cruising up and down the Straits for what seemed like forever.

Battle Station

As a boot, my battle station was on the Superstructure, reporting the exhaust's smoke color, which helped the boiler operators control the fuel mixture. In the old days, dark exhaust could give away your ship's location, but with the advent of radar, the object was to operate the boiler efficiently and not obstruct the pilot's view when landing on the flight deck.

Because I had access to the intercom, I received a lot of information. One thing of note was the pilots were instructed in the event of actual engagement not to return to the ship. She would most likely be destroyed. The Superstructure of a carrier is vulnerable to attack. Being exposed on it, I was very vulnerable. Years later, I learned that Taiwan's F-86 Sabers intercepted a formation of Red Chinese MiG-17s en route to Taiwan, breaking it up with the help of sidewinder AIM-9 Air-to-air missiles, which discouraged further action and likely saved my life.

I've always been lucky that way. It is like I am the seventh son, but then I was only the sixth son. It's not that I wanted to live dangerously. I simply wanted to see what was around the next corner, over the hill, beyond the brick wall. But for many years, I've mulled over those words. The answer is clear; you can see it in every day and in every venue. Everything is a cycle, cycle in cycles, cycles with minuscule to infinite time periods. You cannot escape your cycle, but occasionally, you might get a glimpse into another. Every so often, I believe I get a fleeting glimpse.

Heard You Were Dead, 1959

A year later, I am now going by Bryan, my first name. It's a long story but for now just go with it. I was returning to my ship in San Diego. The year was 1959 and while waiting for a PSA Airlines' Lockheed L-188 Electra flight, San Francisco to San Diego, a luxury item, normally, I would be hitchhiking the return 600-mile trip but thanks to a generous

$14 (ticket price in the day) contribution from my father-in-law, I was taking a flight.

A sailor, in dress-blue uniform, the winter uniform, approached me also and said, "Are you Bryan Farrell?" I went by my first name in the navy. "I heard you were dead, killed hitchhiking. I was surprised and confused and thought about the Twilight Zone. Maybe I did and I'm in a different universe. The cycle in cycle thing."

After a brief period, I replied, "I don't think I'm dead." I thought about it for a moment and continued, "But if that's the case, then we both must be dead and living and meeting in another universe."

The sailor looked confused and a little frightened, and asked, "Are you going to San Diego on flight 45?"

I mockingly replied, "Yes, sir."

We both laughed, mine a legitimate laugh, his sort of uneasy. We were on the same San Diego flight and certainly the same universe, which universe I'm not sure of.

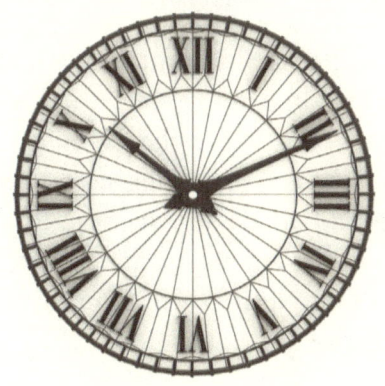

Chapter 7

Escape 1971–2002

Free In My Own Way
Leonard Cohen

For around 40 years, I was a dirt bike rider; it was my escape from the humdrum of urban life, husband, father, day job as a Silicon Valley engineer. I was a late starter, not until I was a bit over 30 did I own my first dirt bike, a Bultaco Alpina, a 250cc two cycle motorcycle (dirt bike). It was not particularly fast, but it was small, light, trackable (go where you pointed it), and maneuverable. Once I became an efficient rider, I loved riding on narrow, demanding dirt trails anywhere, but the high Northern Sierras were my favorite. To be alone, just you, a dirt bike, a loud knob (accelerator) and an unfamiliar trail, who knows what's ahead, an abandoned mine, a forsaken old cabin, a ghost town, or just miles of wind in your face; freedom is something to live for. I had ridden a number of times with other riders, but I loved riding alone, a few hours free, no one to worry about except myself. Yes, riding alone is dangerous, but hell, I've lived on the edge so many times, like hitchhiking in the Navy.

A favorite riding area, Northern California Sierra Gold Country, where old towns like Downieville, Alleghany, and Washington exist.

They were founded during the California Gold Rush, 1849–1858. This gold rush was not the first in America, in 1826 there was a Georgia gold rush, but it was minor compared to the California one. The California gold rush was kicked off by a few gold nuggets found during the building of a sawmill in the South Fork of the American River and exploded into a worldwide gold rush. Thousands of gold seekers of all nationalities poured into the Sierra foothills in search of fortunes.

I have a fondness for towns like Downieville, Alleghany, and Washington because they are almost-has-been-towns, dying slowly but still retaining remnants of their past. There is still life there, working people, original streets, original structure, and great old bars that echo the past, which can be imagined if not experienced and all this among the fragile residue of its past glory.

Downieville, on CA 49, the Gold Chain Highway, a two-lane highway that winds its way through a couple of hundred miles of California's gold mining landscape. Downieville is the county seat of Sierra County and in 1973 there was still a hangman's scaffold in the County's parking lot. Downieville, named after a Major William Downie, honorary title not military rank, led a party of prospectors up the North Yuba River in 1849 and hit paid dirt at the confluence of two rivers, now Yuba and Downie rivers. In 1973, the town was still alive and doing well. It had a couple of restaurants, three bars, some waystations (motel and such), a gas station, a small year-round residents, lots of tourists, and was the county government seat.

Sacramento Daily Union, Volume 82, Number 154, 18 February 1892

Death of the Founder of the Town of Downieville. Major William Downie, after whom the town of Downieville was named, died last week in New Whatcom, Or. He had not been a resident of Downieville for many years, nor anywhere else long at a time. For the last twenty-eight years, he had been a prospector, ranging from Nevada to Alaska. He leaves a wife and children in Oakland. Major Downie came down to the South Fork of the Yuba by the way of Jim Crow Canyon and did his first mining a short distance above Downieville, at 'Hungry Mouth,' taking out gold in large quantities. It was in 1849 that he arrived, among the very first to find their way to the 'Forks' as Downieville was then called. He came out in the good ship, Architect, and lost no time in making his way to the mines. He was an Englishman by birth, upward of 80 years of age (age at the time of his death in 1892). At the time of the hanging of a woman in Downieville, in 1861, the Major had a cabin on the north side of the lower plaza of the town, and it was in this cabin that the woman was confined between her arrest and execution.

Downieville, which is famous for a number of things, but there's one that stands out: the hanging of a young Latino woman, Juanita. She was the first woman hanged in California, 1861. The story has it that Juanita Segovia, in a rage over an incident of the prior night, stabbed a man named Cannon. Juanita must have had a hell of a temper and remained defiant to the end.

Major Downie recounted about the hanging, *"She then took the rope, placed the noose around her neck, said, 'Adiós, señores!' and leaped from the scaffold into eternity."*

I am not sure, but perhaps the rough, abusive environment in the 1861 gold camps in the middle of nowhere might induce a woman to think whatever comes next must be better than this.

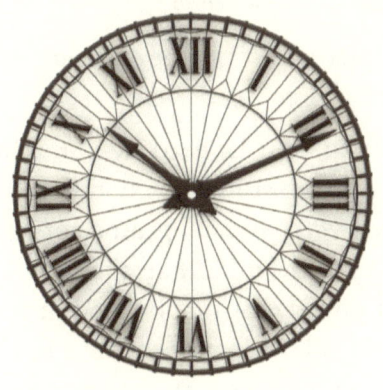

Chapter 8

Theodore Washington Jones
Educated Negro Farmer

First Meeting, Alleghany

It was August 18, 1973, overcast and threatening to rain, my kind of day, turbulent, dicey. I rode out of Downieville on my dirt bike with a full tank of gas, in riding gear, helmet, boots, and gloves. I always rode with a backpack containing tools, rope, compass, and a large garbage bag. I crossed the Yuba rivers on the Nevada St. bridge, past the scaffold and up Gallaway's Grade, a steep winding 6-mile road rising 2500 feet from the Yuba River to the Henness Pass Road—the old main freight route from Marysville to Virginia City. Wow, what exhilaration! A loud knob, good traction, steep, curvy demanding road and me. It is almost like being alive.

My route, Henness Pass Road to Forest, an almost ghost town, was rather smooth but refreshing. It started raining, and I put on my rain gear (a large plastic garbage bag with a hole in it). From Forest, I took Hell's Half Acre, a rather challenging trail in the rain, toward Alleghany, still a mining town in those days. It began to hail about a mile from Alleghany. In those days, Alleghany still had working mines and a number of saloons still operating. One saloon, and the nearest one, was at the foot of the Main St. and Hell's Half Acre Road.

I was wet, shivering, and in need of some shelter. The saloon—I don't remember its name, most likely only history now, like most of the patrons—was crowded with miners, prospectors, and men of all sorts, especially along the bar. In the middle area there was a big black pot belly wood stove. I headed directly for it and stood in front of it, riding gear, helmet, garbage bag and all. At first, the patron just stared at me, kind of surprised by this soaking stranger wearing a garbage bag.

Then half-jokingly, they began interrogating me, "Boy, what the hell you doing out in this weather?"; "Look at what the cat dug in," and so on.

I'd been here before and knew how to handle it. I said, "Hell, I don't have a clue. I am just a dirt bike rider, a pilgrim, a Joseph in need of a shelter."

We started trash talking and laughing together; they started buying me drinks. After a couple of drinks, the new-blood-thing wore off and things quieted down and pretty much went back to normal.

Meeting the Educated Negro Farmer

Too Much Hard Stuff, Perhaps?

I resumed a position in front of the stove and thought about the return trip, over the top of the mountain, at 6500ft elevation, treacherous, dangerous in a hailstorm. I noticed a middle-aged colored man sitting by himself, and it seemed as if we were the only two people there.

I asked, "Do I know you?"

He replied, "You should, Bryan we are related. You are one of the specials, a storyteller. You know the secret. Do not fret, your journey is a long and a safe return trip in this time cycle. But please, come sit here and I'll tell you my story."

I was really surprised he knew my name, I don't remember meeting or talking this rather large black man before and I thought, *how did he know my name, don't think we're related, Secret, damn, I've heard that secret stuff before, but where or when don't know. Okay, I thought, those drinks are getting to me, but I feel good, let's go with it.*

As if a set on the stage of a play had changed, everything seemed different, not totally, but changed.

I sat down across the table and said, "A story, I love stories."

"You know, Bryan, people say the civil war was about State Rights and others say it was about freeing the negroes. I think it was about State Rights, rights to make money they wanted regardless of violating basic human rights. To make it, their economy needed low-cost labor: slaves."

The issue of state rights had been boiling up since the creation of the Union. Now the Southern states had greatly contributed to winning the independents from England and the slavery was mostly an institution. As the abolition movement grew in the Northern State, the Southern States felt they had the right to do just what they wanted, and no damn northern busy body had the right to tell them how to live. Be it as it may, it was bloody and one hell of a mess; I know firsthand.

"Well, thanks for the enlightenment, and how did you know my name?" I replied.

"Oh, I've heard about you. You know the secret," he replied.

"Damn, what secret? I keep hearing about a secret but don't know any secrets. There is none I want to share," I said.

"This is not the place or the time, but I'm here to tell you my story," was his reply.

"My Christian name is Theodore Washington Jones. I was a free negro farming a section of land in the state of Ohio back in '61, that's 1861, when all this Confederacy stuff boiled over. I was not born free; my father was a plantation owner somewhere in Georgia and my mother was one of his slaves. Well, as I was told; when my father, Mr. Abraham Davis Jones, was nearing his death, he had recurring nightmares about hell, of eternal damnation and believed his immortal soul was damned and the only way to save it was to free his slaves. Being a free negro at any time in the deep South was tenuous, but in the 1840s it was damn right dangerous. The bounty for an escaped slave was $500 per head and to tell the truth, bounty hunters did not much care if you were a free negro or not, that you were a negro was enough. To top it off, I was very young, just a half-black child. As luck would have it, the local Presbyterian Minister, Mr. John Joseph Wields, an abolitionist, was asked by the church elders to leave, well, aggressively encouraged, forced out of his post there and agreed to minister a new church in Ohio, not much more than a frontier west of the Appellations. Miss Lavina Mogertte Jones, my white sister, well, half-sister, and your grandmother's cousin."

Grandmother? I hardly knew anything about my grandmother and nothing of her cousin other than she comes from a prominent southern family. How could he know?

"She took pity, understood my plight, and convinced Mr. Wields of the need to get me north of the Mason-Dixson line. Mr. Wields not only transported me to Ohio, but he also raised and provided me an education.

"While Mr. Wields was, in fact, a de facto foster father, he insisted I addressed him as Mr. Wields, never as dad. While he believed he was doing God's work, shielding and raising an unwanted negro child, he wanted to make it clear that he was not my biological father. I can't help but think that he thought God's work included having me follow a righteous path and becoming the first ordained black Presbyterian Minister. But I could not reconcile his caring, loving, forgiving God with the God I knew who would allow such things as enslaving people. Perhaps his God would allow slavery only if the enslaved people were black. So instead, I chose to do God's work, farming a section of land in southeast Ohio, not sure it's God's work but farming provides a measure of isolation, mostly free from the probing eyes, eyes beyond to the curious mass. *'A negro who can read? Do you think he can write? Does not talk like other niggers.'* Instead of becoming the first black Presbyterian Minister, I became, as the locals call me, *'that educated nigger farmer.'* One thing is for sure, their prejudices did not stop them from seeking my help in reading letters for them, translating legal notices, or advising on the best way to castrate a ram. But then there were the neighbors who came to my aid during a slave pirate raid.

"You see, Bryan, slave pirates—as the locals called them—were unsavory men who captured black men, women, children and sold them in the slave markets. One well-known group from Kentucky, a neighboring slave state, had made three successful raids up north. Runaway or free did not matter. There was a market for any healthy blacks. Local rumor has it that they planned a fourth raid, their last, they bragged, to fund the trip to California's gold country.

There were a number of holes in the plan, but the biggest was their big mouths. The first target was that educated nigger farmer just across the state line, they boasted, to not only make some money but to also get rid of a dangerous educated negro. Word got out that those Kentucky boys were in the area. I was preparing a reception for them, if they thought this educated nigger farmer was going down without a fight, they were in for a surprise. I had weapons and was a damn good shot.

"In the morning, the geese down by the creek were raising a commotion, always a sign someone was coming. It was Mr. Ludwick, a new neighbor. I'd heard that the Wrights had sold their section to an ex-military man. I saw him crossing the creek and heading directly towards the house. Still wearing his old army trousers, rather worn and faded, but you could still distinguish the union blue. He looked directly at me, tilted his head slightly and said, 'He and his two brothers were going to help. First thing is to set up a defensible line between the creek and the house and have it well stocked with weapons and ammunition. These boys are dangerous, and I believe they are out to prove a point. They're confederate sympathizers and might be working with the local rebels.' He continued, 'Did you hear our local Union Militia retook control of the arsenal in St. Louis? They arrested the bunch of rebel sympathizers and marched them right through the city streets. No free negroes, that's what those boys want, that's why you are targeted. If we just scare them off, they might well just return when you're alone. You need to shoot to kill. Can you do that?'

"Kill, kill another human. I thought, *don't know if I can. Hell, I felt sorry for the jack rabbits I killed as a kid. Just learning to hunt, practicing shooting jack rabbits to improve aim, but always felt sorry for the rabbit that was in the wrong place at the wrong time. Now, I may have to kill another human just because I am in the wrong place at the wrong time. Hell, I'm probably in the wrong century, an educated nigger.*

"I told Mr. Ludwick, I do not understand the whole thing, these northern white people, abolitionists, causing the country to tear itself apart to abolish slavery. What can they gain? Oh, I can understand southern people, slavery, a necessary ingredient in their economy. Well, that is, those rich southern white people. I did not understand those white-trash, southern poor men. Why would they risk their lives to protect slavery?

"Then I looked at Mr. Ludwick. He did not look like a military man, and he did not ride a horse like a military man. He kind of slouched in the saddle. And then, as if someone else was speaking, I said, 'I do not believe those men would dare come by and try to kidnap me. I can take care of myself.' He looked surprised and offended at my reply. I am not sure if it was the flawless English with a slight hint of New England accent or the content of my reply, but he gave me a look of disbelief and said, 'To each his own,' turned his horse and rode off.

"I sat in a stupor thinking, how stupid, refusing help I desperately needed. Do I think just because I am educated, I can outsmart those scoundrels, hell's bells, they make a living seizing black men. They may have no schooling, but they have plenty of backwoods training".

"Then, for some reason, my thoughts turned to Elisabeth Warren, one of my neighbors, just down the road a mile or so toward the Ohio river. She was a young widow whose husband contracted typhoid during a business trip. She had been a widow now for two years, an appropriate grieving period and acceptable to remarry. She'd been looking for a mate, well, ever since the death of her husband, without success. Most of the eligible men were looking for a rich widow, someone who could enhance their financial status. Beth, the name she preferred, I knew could not consider me. I was a negro but I could tell she thought I was attractive, six feet tall, broad shoulders, fine facial features with my beautiful white teeth and chocolate colored skin. Truth be told, I was probably one of the smartest males in the county. Now, while her intention was simply to be neighborly, her visits were so regular and often that the whole county had taken note."

""Well Bryan", he continued, "you see now, I had two items to worry about: slave traders and my woman neighbor, Elisabeth Warren. The other day, I overheard some of the local women at the market talking about the widow Mrs. Warren and how often she visited that educated negro. I had also taken notice and was concerned for my wellbeing. My god, I thought, this will not stand. A black man involved with a white woman. Not even in Ohio,, a state above the Mason Dixon Line. I don't think Mr. John Joseph Wield's forgiving God would tolerate this and damn sure the white males would not tolerate this, a threat to their manhood, to their superiority, and they would act violently. A hanging would be in order. It seems I now had two problems, possibly being abducted and sold into slavery or being severely beaten and then hung.

"That evening, the geese raised a commotion. I hoped it was just a fox or something, but no, I heard the hoofs then, footsteps rushing towards the house. I picked up my long rifle and peeked out the gun slot, a remnant of the Indian raids years ago. I did not recognize the white man on the porch.

"'Theodore, I am a neighbor. No time to waste. You've got to get the hell out of here!' he shouted.

"I was not sure if this was just a ploy to get me outside or what, so I shouted back, 'What's the big rush?'

"I still did not recognize the man.

"'There's a bunch of riled up men heading this way, maybe ten minutes behind me. They got hanging on their minds, think you shot a kid the other night, been frolicking with and courting white women. No time, just get out of here, use the River Road south toward the Ohio river. They will think you're headed north. I'll ride in that direction, leaving a trail. Come on boy, high tail it.'

"I cried out, 'Who you calling boy?' *Not going to allow that*, I thought.

"'God dammit, boy, don't start with that bullshit. I only meant to save your black ass. It doesn't make any difference to me. Now get your horse, don't have time to saddle it, just ride bareback due south. Can you do that?' he shouted back.

"I was sure if I opened the door, all hell would break loose; it was a set-up. I didn't say a word, just went directly to the trapdoor in the hallway floor and escaped out the back. Through the evening light, I could just make out a group, 12 or 15 men, standing not more than twenty feet off the porch. It was just dark enough for me to crawl a 100 or so yards undetected, get to my feet, still undetected, and run to the path leading through the grove of cottonwood trees, boarding the River Road.

"I started to head down the road when I heard a voice, 'Get your damn black ass off the road, don't you know nothing? First place they be looking, fool.' A young man, a black man, said as he grabbed and forcefully pulled me off the road into the ditch along side of the road.

"'Need to stay hidden, tell dark,' he said. 'Shush, I hear something up the road," he said.

"I started to ask what, but with conviction and fear the man clamped his hand over my mouth. Almost at the same moment, a number of horse-mounted men stopped directly across the path, the escape path I'd just used.

"I could see two men dismounting and heard a mounted man say, 'Stay here, Jeff and Horace, watch for that negro, he can't be far.'

"He seemed to be in charge.

"They were so close I could hear them talking.

"'Yes, ya, ya,' a much younger man, more like a boy, replied. 'Why you give me shitty jobs?' he added.

"'Cause, Jeff, you're just a kid and that's why,' the mounted men said as he rode off.

"'Let's walk up that path a bit and hide,' the other man, just a boy but a head taller than the other boy, said. 'That way, we can get the drop on the negro.'

"'Hell, Horace, I hope that neger doesn't come this way,' the other boy replied. 'The last thing I want to do is shoot him. I hope he gets away, that he makes it up north. Hell, that's where I'm heading soon as I get a chance. I'm getting one of those factory jobs up north. They say they pay real well.'

"'Shit, boy,' the tall boy said in a righteous tone, 'I did not know you were a neger lover.'

"'God damn it, Horace, time is changing, this slavery, plantation stuff has got to go, that's what my teacher says, and I think he's right,' the boy sneered back.

"'Well, my Pa,' the tall boy replied, 'Says this is the way God meant it to be. The white man is superior, and the black man needs looking after.'

"'Well, Horace, you can look after the black man. I'm going north and getting far away from this superior stuff. There's going to be a lot of killing and I'm damn sure I don't want to die, superior or not,' the smaller boy replied as they disappeared into the woods, still gibbering and horsing around."

"As soon as we figured those white boys were safely out of hearing range, the young black man nudged me and started crawling down the ditch, putting some distance between them and the mob. We hightailed it for a grove of Betula trees just off the road a few hundred feet and settled down there to wait out the mob. For the first time, I realized how big a man he was. He was a head taller than me and all muscle and bone.

"I asked his name, and he replied, 'Moses, I'm a runaway. People have been helping me to escape; they were going to meet me in the morning and help me get up north,' he said. Then he stopped and looked at me and said, 'You talk like white folks, are you that educated negro farmer?'

"Does everyone know about me, I thought.

'Yes,' I replied.

"After Moses stared at me for a moment. 'Better not let white folks know you are educated; they'll hang you for sure,' he said.

"It was Not long after we hid in the Betula grove, I could hear the mob return to collect the two posted boys. After a few minutes, they rode off in a northern direction, most likely heading for Red's, the nearest tavern, to brag about running off that educated nigger.

"I must have fallen asleep and awoke to the sound of Red-Headed Woodpeckers scrounging for their breakfast. I had no idea where I was, but knew I was not in my bed. I hurt all over and knew I'd spent the night sleeping on the ground. After a moment, I noticed a man, a large black man, standing on the edge of the Betula grove. He seemed to be watching, observing the area. Then the memory, the nightmare of the events of the prior evening came screaming back, hiding with Moses and all. What a mess, I thought. *I'm between a rock and a hard spot, a mob wanting to hang me, slave pirates wanting to capture me, can't go home and nowhere to run.*

"Moses turned, looked at me and said, 'Hear people coming south on the road, think it might be the people helping me run away.' He continued, 'Supposed to rendezvous this morning.'

"He started walking toward the road, and I followed, thinking I had nowhere else to go. They were near the edges of the grove when two white men riding mules rode past. After a little bit, Moses started down the road waving his arms to attract their attention. Then, to our surprise, a young man came trotting down the road.

"He started yelling, 'Aaron, Adam, the negroes are down here.'

"The two men turned around and rode directly toward us. One of the men had a rifle at the ready and he was shouting to lie down on the road."

"Well, Bryan, those Lynch boys thought their plan was going smoothly, but as you know, they don't always work out. The pirate's plans were one of these; just as those Lynch boys were sure they had pulled it off and heading for New Orleans with us, Moses and me, to sell, we ran into a bunch of rebel soldiers going somewhere.

"A man, the only man in a gray and blue Confederate uniform, said, 'Where you-all going?' in a commanding tone, with a Georgian accent.

"One of them, the youngest boy I think, replied, 'To the slave market in Orleans to sell these runaway slaves. Then we're going to California.'

"The older boy groaned, and gave him the look, 'You are as stupid as you look.'

"'Well, boys, do you have ownership papers for that property?' the uniformed man asked.

"The boys looked at each other and said, 'We captured these runaway slaves and are just returning them.'

"'Do you have the warrants?' he asked.

"'No, sir, but we captured these runaways and intend to sell them at the market,' the older boy replied.

"The head man in uniform looked at his men and nodded his head and said, 'Sergeant.'

"Without another word, a rather large man with messy red hair, even redder beard and intense eyes, stepped forward, spit a mouth full of chewing tobacco and grabbed their mules' reins. 'Now here's where we are boys. You are in possession of stolen property, and it is my duty as an officer of the state of Kentucky to enforce its law. I am confiscating the property and arresting you two boys. The other boy is a kid and can't be held responsible. I can either just hang you two or the other option is you enlist in the Army of Tennessee for ninety days and I will not ask you again,' he said.

"Two boys nodded yes, almost in unison and said, 'Yes, sir.'

"The officer looked at the younger boy and asked, "Boy, what's your name?'

"'Azriell Thomas Lynch, given name, but I am called Tommy sir.'

"'Well, son, Azriell Thomas Lynch, can either go your way or tag along with us as a soldier. You two,'—looking at Moses and me—, said, 'Get in line with the other slaves. You are now property of the army of Kentucky.'"

So, Bryan for about a year I was a slave, I went from having a name, Theodore Washington Jones, the Educated Negro Farmer, to, 'You neger or black man. Get over there and help get that wagon out of the mud.'

"I thought, *I could not believe how badly things had gone the past seven months*, as I trudged along in the rain alongside thirty slaves, somewhere in Kentucky, not knowing where I am going or why. Now, just part of a slave work crew supporting the confederate war effort. My clothes are rags, I was dirty head to toe, and I was half starved.

"I was treated like an animal, no different from a common mule, just not as stubborn. One thing for sure, the head sergeant boss man did not hesitate to use the whip, and I learned to say, 'Yes um, boss.'

"About this time, I thought, *I might have been better off letting that mob hang me, hell I'll probably die of hunger or be killed by some stray bullet, anyway.*

What in the hell were those slave pirates doing riding down the River Road that morning, just as Moses and I thought we'd escaped the mob, I can't figure it?. The only good thing is those pirates, all three of them, volunteered, forced might be a better description, to enlist in the Confederate Army, kinda poetic justice, and just as likely to get killed as I am. In a way, those pirates were fortunate to avoid that mob in Ohio, people in Ohio don't cotton to Kentucky slave pirates. Those Kentucky slave pirate's lot were not much better than us slaves. Most of the time, they were working alongside us."

"In early October, the army of Tennessee, soldiers, and slaves alike began moving, rather urgently in a southern direction, I knew it was southern, being a farmer, I was acutely aware of direction, supposedly, we were heading for some camp to reinforce the garrison there. It seems the Yankees were intent on taking control of it. A battle, I learned later, was called the Battle of Camp Wildcat, started early in the morning, at first a skirmish and then grew into a full fledge battle by midday. Wounded men were streaming in, some bad, some not so bad and some just scared. This war stuff was dangerous and not much glory. I was glad we colored were not supposed to fight. One thing for sure, the white folks did not want us blacks to learn how to fight.

"As the battle continued, the day turned hot and muggy. Moses and I were sitting among a grove of laurel trees, trying to be invisible, not far from a temporary holding pen for the cavalry horses. It was hot, muggy, smelled like horse shit, infested with flies, but it was as far from the sound of the battle as we could get. We tried to be sitting away from the rest of the slaves, always making plans to escape. A surgeon doctor spotted us and directed a nurse to have those colored boys, pointing at us, help bring in the wounded. The doctor was totally overwhelmed, wounded men, mourning, dying, and crying for their mothers were everywhere. I had learned about human anatomy and some rudimental medical procedures as part of my preparation for ministry. I would have gone on a mission to help the needy and spread the faith, most likely the Sandwich Islands.

"I had no sympathy for these wounded, they were my adversary, my enemy, my captors but when I saw a very young, badly wounded boy laying off to the side, seemingly left to die, alone and dying, his hand partially blown off, clearly bleeding to death, even loathing the whole war thing and especially the whites, I grabbed a strip of cloth, tied it about his wrist, the bleeding slowed.

"The doctor looked at me. He realized I knew what I was doing, that I had some training in the medical area. He said, 'Bring that patient here.'

"I replied, 'Yes sum.'

"He looked at me and said, 'don't speak colored talk. I know you have been trained in medical treatment and I suspect you can speak white folk's English.'

"*My god*, I thought, *how stupid of me, now I've lost my invisibility.*

"Then he said, 'You'd be that educated negro farmer I've heard about.'

I thought, *My god, does everybody know about me?*

The surgeon must have been someone with high-level connections. When the boss sergeant saw me in the medical tent, he shouted, 'Get your raggy black ass out here and go with the slaves. You needed to repair our works!'

"The surgeon ordered me to stay, insisting I was needed here and more valuable to the war effort assisting with the wounded than working on the work gang. The next hour or so, casualties poured in, many so badly wounded they could not be saved. It was hot and muggy, the air was filled with the smell of blood, death and flies swarmed about me. I was covered with other men's blood; my soul was hurting, and it forced me to question the very existence of mankind. I was tired of the blood, the crying, the screams of pain, the destruction of human bodies. Men, who in another circumstance would not even speak to me, now hung onto me, imploring me to help them. They were my enemy, my oppressors, but I was doing whatever I could to save their lives, relieve their pain. But instinctively I understood why, it was not for them, it was for myself. I was no longer a man, just a slave, but I would not allow my antagonist to dehumanize my soul."

Theodore looked up at the ceiling, then at me and said "Exodus A Free Man Again" he paused for along moment and continued "It was

October in Kentucky I remember, the days were getting short, the summer heat was still stiflingly hot but would soon giveaway to a cooler autumn and autumn colors. The bright red cardinals would stop by the creek on their return trip to Mexico. Oh, how I wish I was migrating on my way to somewhere else. I began to think about the fall harvest, forgetting I was a captive slave in the middle of a raging battle. The sounds of battle continued unabated, were closer and closer and then, without warning, all hell seemed to break loose. Men, some in gray tattered uniform, rifles slung over their shoulders, some in partial uniform, dragging their rifles, some in ragged civilian clothes, without weapons, began streaming past the medical tent shouting, 'Yankees are coming, lines broken, got to get out of here.'

"The doctor looked around, said 'Be calm, you all, the Yankees will respect the medical people, they are not interested in us.' Looking at me, he said, 'You stay put, it is going to be dangerous out there.'

"Soldiers in blue uniforms began streaming through the area, some stopping and peering into the medical tent, one carrying a badly wounded soldier came in, looked at the doctor and said, 'My mate here is badly wounded, please look after him.'

"The doctor looked at me, said, 'Boy, see to it, help that wounded man.'

"As I took the wounded man from the soldier, anxiety in his face gave way to a look of hope. With tears streaming down his face, he said, 'Thank you.'

"I was surprised how light the wounded man was. His uniform, made with home-woven cloths and hand stitching, most likely made by his mother, had absorbed a great deal of blood. His young face was filled with pain. He opened his eyes, looked at me, I could see eternity looking back at me. He closed his eyes, the pain softened into a peaceful, content look, and he was dead. But I did not let his buddy know, instead I carried him over and laid him on a cot. How young they were, how stupid to risk they lives, for what? To save a nation, to free the slaves, for what? I could take it no longer. I turned and headed straight out of the tent in the directions the Yanks were coming. Dangerous or not, I was a free man again, and I was going where I damn well felt like.

"I was heading north, or at least in the direction the union soldiers were coming from, when a mounted soldier, and officer I think, hollered, 'Theodore, what on God's green earth are you doing here? How in the hell do you end up here?'

"It was my neighbor from Ohio, the one that offered me help. I thought, *Hell, I did not want his help then and I don't now.*

"He said something about some good news and if I meet him later, he will help me get out of Kentucky. Then I thought, *Maybe I better wait and find out about the good news and accept his offer to help me get out of this mess.*"

"The good news was my property in Ohio had been sold and the money was being held by a trust company and I could claim it.

"Lieutenant Ludwick explained, 'Mr. Jones, when you were absent for three months, you were declared missing and the property was sold by the county and money held by a trust, $1000.'

"*Great*, I thought, that money I can use to invest in land when I get to California. But he also had some bad news. He'd been ordered elsewhere and could not assist my exodus out of this god-forsaken Kentucky. He would look for help, perhaps another outfit would be going north, and they could get me out of this slave state.

"The more I thought about it, the more I wanted to help fight those damned rebels. To my surprise, I said, 'I would like a chance to help defeat the Confederacy.'

"After a moment of silence, the lieutenant, the first white person in Kentucky to address me as a man, an equal, said he believed I could possibly help as an adviser, with my education I could do many of the tasks that an adjutant would do and right now the Union was really short in manpower. But it would be very dangerous being a colored man working with Yankees. It was a death sentence if the confederacy captured me. He knew me as the educated negro farmer, but I don't think he knew how extensive my education had been. I was proficient in not only language and mathematics but also in warfare history. One of my teachers had been in the military, a graduate of West Point. He taught me mathematics, surveying and the history of military maneuvers."

Help fight, I am not a soldier I'm a farmer "But after I cooled down. I thought, Hell, those confederates' son-of-a-bitches are not going to treat me like a dog and get away with it, I am going to fight back anyway I can. So, I joined the Union Army to do whatever I could to help.

"So, Bryan." he said" looking at me. I was startled back to the present and somewhat confused, so engrossed with his story I'd forgotten I was sitting in a bar listening to a narrative of some long ago and mostly unimportant event.

"That's how I, an Educated Negro," he continued "a black man, was one of the first black men to be in the Union Army, the Mississippi army. It's getting late and you need to get going on your ride over the mountain. Someday, we will meet again. You see, our cycle seems to be aligned in such a way they entangle. Oh, before you go, take this book,"— he handed me a small black leather-bound notebook with LL initials embedded on it—"Better put it in your backpack or you might lose it on you return. Oh, and may luck be with you, not many special people do dumb risky things, like riding alone in a hailstorm."

Better To Be Lucky Than Good

And I needed luck that night, wearing my garbage bag rain gear, slightly toasted, I retraced my route through Forest to Henness Pass Road to Dog Valley Road to the unmarked Y in the Gallaway grade, about half a mile from the intersection with Dog Valley Road. It was nearly dark, raining with hail, running low on fuel and I had to make a decision: Which road? But I could not quite recall which one. A wrong decision could be lethal. I chose the right-hand road, felt Downeville had to be off to the right. As I neared the point-of-no-return, fuel issue, I looked over the edge of the trail and saw Downeville's lights a thousand or so feet below, yes, I'd chosen the right road, Gallaway for sure. I gratefully proceeded to cruise down Gallaway's Grade past the hangmen's noose in the county's lot, across the Yuba River bridge, into my night's lodging parking area, wet, cold, needing shelter.

Grateful to be out of the elements, in a warm comfortable lodging, I proceeded to bed, after shedding the garbage bag, riding gear, and my wet clothes.

I thought I'd slept soundly, but in the morning, the events of the preceding day flooded back into my consciousness. I thought I must have had dreamed the whole thing, but then; I check my backpack and there it was, a small black leather-bound notebook, LL printed on the cover.

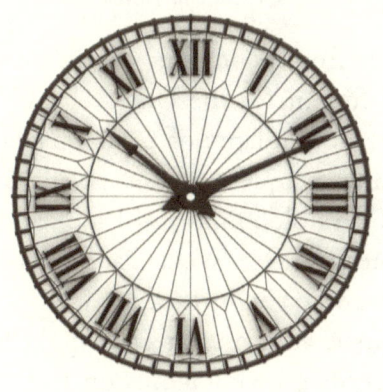

Chapter 9

Lieutenant Ludwick
A Soldier's Life, 1846, Ohio

After breakfast at the Forks, the best tavern in town, well, the only tavern but still a good breakfast, I took a seat on the edge of Yuba River, just past the bridge. I knew subconsciously I wanted to check out the small, black leather-bound notebook with LL printed on the cover, but consciously, I was frightened. The whole thing yesterday was quite overwhelming and the memory of that hitchhiking ride with a want-to-be lieutenant years ago in my Navy days reverberated in my mind. But deny it or not, I knew I would read it. The notebook read more like a novel than a journal and I felt it was meant to be, a long-gone Union soldier's story.

The note book, more like a journal, quite nicely made, great condition to be 100 years old, seemed like it has not weather since the Lieutenant's days. The first paragraph addressed the closing of the 1846 Mexican war. It read as follows: After the Mexican War victory the Union army was reduced to a peacetime level, all the volunteers were dismissed and even many of the regular army were furloughed or resigned their commission. boredom, and low pay were the main causes. I was a First Lieutenant in the regular army, I decided to resigned my commission to be with my family back in Ohio. I was a professional soldier, a West

Point graduate. I came from a long line of soldiering people, my father, and grandfather had fought for the Union. Family lore has it that the Ludwicks were direct descendants of Charlemagne, the Frank warrior that halted the Mores's conquest of Europe. But my mother said the warriors were from Dad's bloodline and I looked more like her family. They have been farmers forever. Well, Dad got me an appointment to West Point and off I went to try my luck as a warrior. I did well there, and I had intended to pursue an army career. I might be a warrior at heart, but could not support my growing family on army pay.

Resigned Commission

I resigned my commission and returned to my hometown to open a dry goods store. It turned out I was a good businessman and successful. I had purchased a section of land near the Ohio river and had my brothers farming it. I really did not expect the slave issue to gravitate to the point of southern state succession. With the election of Abraham Lincoln, a number of Southern States panicked over the abolition issue. Foolish young men began amassing into pro confederate or pro Union groups. Just last week, a group of confederate sympathizers took control of the armory in St Louis. When a local unionist showed up with weapons loaded and ready, the confederates surrendered without a shot. Talk of war was everywhere: tavern, church, stage stop, and street corner. Of course, those that would not have to fight, the old, the lame, the dumb were the loudest. I refused to participate in the discussion; they had no idea what war really meant. The majority would run for shelter at the sign of a real battle, bullets flying, bloody and dying men everywhere. No, I've been there and know what war looks, smells and tastes like.

Not For War, 1861

I was not for war. I had been trained for and participated in war, hoped it would not come to that, but I was not going to allow the disintegration of the Union, not if I could help it.

I did not want to leave my family again, but I intended to serve my country in the capacity I was trained for, a professional soldier, and I would pay whatever personal cost. It troubled me, that rebels' nonsense about the northerners not having the guts to fight, that was dangerous thinking, underestimating your foe. Just ask General Antonio López de Santa Anna. In the battle of San Jacinto, he totally underestimated the Texans and lost half of Mexico and damn near his life. He betrayed Mexico, signing a land giveaway to save his life.

But it is clear the Union was not taking the succession talk seriously, thinking the south could not sustain a war and would capitulate after their first battle. No, Jefferson Davis, and the other traitors had been planning, conspiring for the succession.

Hell, the secretary of war, John B. Floyd, had manipulated the military in order to weaken the Union Army. He should have been arrested and thrown into jail. I had been sitting on the fence regarding becoming a soldier again; did not want to leave my family, but confederate rebels taking over the Armory in St. Louis was the deciding event. If we were not careful, Ohio could slide into the confederacy. I had heard that Sherman had accepted the command of the Ohio State Militia and was in the process of building a staff. I had never met Lieutenant Sherman. Although we had both served in the Mexican War and both West Point graduates; our paths had never crossed. I decided to write to him and offer him my service. He sent his adjutant to meet me in Lexington.

He, the adjutant, handed me an acceptance letter and a set of orders to hook up with and take command of the Portsmouth Home Guard. I was confused and disappointed. I had expected more, a member of his staff or at least a company commander. After all, I was a West Point graduate, experienced veteran First Lieutenant. I thought about forgetting the whole thing; the weather was stormy, it would be a tough, miserable trip to Portsmouth, but to tell the truth deep inside, the thought of being a warrior again excited me.

The adjutant could see the disappointment on my face, and said, "Portsmouth is strategically important because it blocks the northern invasion route into Ohio. The Home Guard militia there is the first line of defense. This is an important assignment and a path for you into Sherman's command."

Portsmouth Militia, Scioto County, Ohio, 1861

This soldiering thing is about trust. Trust your fellow soldier will cover your back and will not break and run in the heat of battle. Armies are all about orderly discipline and control. I had never been involved with a militia before or had to deal with raw recruits.

To my surprise, this unit had been organized by an ex-union sergeant, Kelly, a wiry, redheaded veteran who had resigned during the Seminole Wars in protest. He emigrated to America to escape poverty and the virtual enslavement of the Gaelic-speaking people by the English Crown. He wanted no part of stealing the Indians' land and shipping them off to the Indian territory.

Kelly disdained those abolitionists who only talked about abolishing slavery. He was going to do something about it. He had organized and trained the Portsmouth militia in fundamental military marching maneuvers. Then a young West Point graduate, Second Lieutenant Sheetz, had joined the Militia and was now serving on my staff, well, the only one on my staff. He was a godsend, a genius in logistics. He managed to procure essential military equipment, tents, backpacks, socks, weapons, munition, boots for the unit. He'd arranged the transportation for the militia. Food provisions were acquired locally. The men acquired their uniforms from local women volunteers that hand stitched and used home-weaved cloth. By the end of September '61, we were a respectable fighting unit, a platoon of 34 men and officers.

The Confederate forces were becoming active in Kentucky, an effort to control the Mississippi River. Brig. General Grant countered by moving in additional Union forces to reinforce strategically important areas. I was ordered to move the Portsmouth Militia into Kentucky to reinforce the Union force at Camp Wildcat. While it was only a platoon, reinforcement was sorely needed to counter a move by confederate general Zollicoffer's 11th Tennessee Infantry moving against the Louisville & Nashville Railroad, a major supply route for the Union Army. If the union force that Camp Wildcat could be routed, the path to the railroad would be clear. There was no railroad from Portsmouth to the camp, so the platoon would have to march the 90-miles through confederate sympathetic territory. Making it difficult to procure food, to bivouac, to get directions and there's a real possibility of being bushwhacked on the way.

Although it was well known that this region of Kentucky was sympathetic toward the Southerner, there were a number of Union supporters there. Word got out about my platoon marching through, the union supporters organized and provided support. They not only helped with food supplies but also direction. There were several deep creeks to be forged on the way. They, the union supporters, directed the platoon to the best fords and even assisted in the crossing. It became clear to me how divisive and bloody this war would be, neighbors and even family divided against each other.

Camp Wildcat Battle

October 18, 1861

After three days of forced marching and many creek crossings, we reached Camp Wildcat. The battle had already started, the confederate's initial attack at Round Hill had failed. They had regrouped and were attacking with a larger force, a few thousand men, including 12th and 17th Tennessee Infantry. They were attacking at a place called the South Rim, not far from the Round Hill battle site. The Union force had fortified their position, holding on, but outnumbered and were close to being over ran. As reinforcements poured in, including the Portsmouth Home Guard, the Union straightened their lines. A lieutenant who seemed in charge or just took control directed my platoon to the western end of the palisade. As we approached the works, it was apparent the confederates had just broken through. Sergeant Kelly instinctively ordered the men to charge. The rebel force was totally surprised, turned and ran in disorder back over the bulwark in full retreat.

Finds Mr. Jones

The in-charged lieutenant had observed the action, began clapping his hands and gave the old Roman thumbs up sign. The union soldiers gave chase and followed the retreating confederate about a quarter of a mile past a tent, a confederate medical tent. I was mounted on a borrowed horse and rode behind the charging union men; I notice a negro man walking straight in my direction. He seemed impervious to all the commotion as the union soldiers charged past him. He was wearing ragged work clothes and looked like so many of the newly freed slaves here in the area. But as he looked at me, I recognized him, my neighbor, the Educated Negro Farmer. I said, "Theodore Washington Jones, how are you? What on god's green earth are you doing here?"

At first, he did not recognize me, and he must have wondered how I knew his name, then he remembered the ex-soldier neighbor, took a long look and then replied in a calm voice, "I thought I might just take an afternoon stroll, Lieutenant Ludwick. I am getting out of here, out of Kentucky, out of this damn war."

I was surprised he knew my name and rank. "Mr. Jones," I said, "Kentucky is a dangerous place right now, especially for a black man. I suggest staying put in this area with the Yankees. I have some good news for you and perhaps I can help you get out of Kentucky. Right now, I've got a battle to fight and a platoon to look after."

August 29–30, 1862

Battle for Richmond Kentucky

I was proud of my platoon, the Portsmouth Home Guard. They had endured a demanding forced march through foul weather, unfriendly territory, and fought together as a unit during the battle. The Lieutenant in charge, Braidy, an aide to Brigadier General Manson, visited my camp that evening to commend my actions during the battle and hand me new orders. I had planned to return to Portsmouth with the platoon and also convoy Theodore out of Kentucky, but now I had orders to proceed to Richmond Kentucky to join General Manson, the commander of the Union forces in that area. The lieutenant had recommended me for a promotion to a regular army lieutenant and I had been assigned to command a company of infantry. The men of Portsmouth Home Guard volunteered to join my new command for 90 days.

I had to break the news to Theodore. I would not be able to convoy him out of Kentucky and that I would look for help here because it was too dangerous for him to proceed on his own.

Theodore's reaction surprised me. He looked away for a moment and said, "Lieutenant, is there any way I can help? I am willing to take up arms and fight alongside you wherever, however."

I told him "I do not know what the status is regarding negro serving in the army, I am sure it is only a matter of time before negro men will be allowed to fight but, in the meantime, I would be glad to have you as an adviser, I believe you will be a real asset, with your education and experience."

After getting a quasi-approval from Captain Harrich, I agreed to have Theodore as my unofficial adjutant since he could not be enlisted. I thought he would make a fine adjutant, official or unofficial, but first, I needed to get him out of those raggy clothes. I had heard of a tailor's shop in Logan's Crossroads still in business, so I arranged to have him fitted with a new civilian outfit. But as it turns out, Theodore got more than just a fresh set of clothes. As I understand it, a simple tailoring job turn into a fiasco with some confederate soldiers trying to capture my men and Mr. Jones. I heard that half twit Lynch boy was involved, and that shots were fired with one casualty, a young negro girl. My men started laughing as they described the rebels chasing their runaway mules hauling a loaded wagon.

On a cool morning, the first of September 1862, my new company, and staff, including Mr. Jones, began a 35-mile march north eastward towards Richmond, Kentucky. The Union force at Big Hill did not fare well there; we had to make a hasty retreat. Theodore remained cool in battle and contributed to an orderly withdrawal and was a major factor in keeping Portsmouth Home Guard in order. He became an official union soldier. In 1862, President Lincoln's Emancipation Proclamation enabled African Americans to enlist in the Union Army. He continued as my adjutant, nearly to war's end. After the union victory at Atlanta Mr. Jones asked to relieved of this duties as my adjutant and requested to be mustard out of the army. I saw him to the steamer, bided him farewell and told him I hoped to see him again in California.

After reading the lieutenant's journal, I, Bryan could not help wonder why would a soldier write a war journal about such a narrow subject , not about the many battles on the road to Atlanta or many other war events but then again I had no way explaining the event of the last couple of days so I rationalized it is just one more of the twilight zone things.

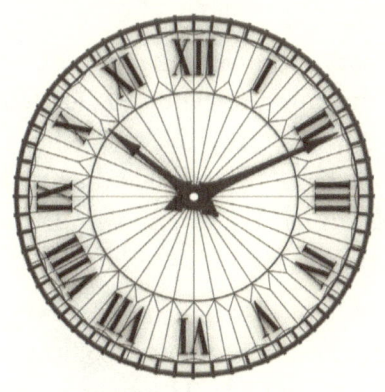

Chapter 10

Twilight Zone
California, 1947–1984

Sometimes, there is an event I cannot quite understand or explain. Things in my life that leave me thinking maybe there is something other than Newtonian physics ruling daily life. In that case, I relegate it to a twilight zone thing.

I was fifteen. I'd purchased a 1948 metallic green Mercury with money earned from my dishwashing job at Lincoln golf course. Being fifteen, I could only get a learner's permit and was required to have a licensed driver accompany me. My friend, Stan, was sixteen and had a driver's license. I had a car and Stan had a license, so we decided to skip school and go to Santa Cruz. On the return trip, there was a near collision, or maybe a collision, between my 1948 metallic green Mercury and a big gray Greyhound Bus. The reason it was a near collision and not a collision is there was no physical damage, but how my Mercury and I escaped is a mystery. It seemed at the time that there was no escaping a head on collision. I and two passengers, Stan, my best friend and a young hitchhiker I'd picked up in Santa Cruz, were on Highway 9 heading for Los Gatos. In the day, Highway 9 over the coast mountain was a three-lane road, the center lane for passing. I was in the passing lane, passing a car, when a car coming in the opposite direction also used that lane. To avoid a head-on collision, I reacted by pulling into the third lane, which was occupied by an oncoming Greyhound Bus. The next thing I knew was that somehow, I'd avoided the bus and other cars and was back in the proper lane, free and clear, flying down the Santa Cruz Hi-Way. But I do not know how, cannot recall how and wonder what really happened. I was not sure if me and my friends were in the same universe or what.

A similar thing happened years later while riding out of Alleghany on route to Washington; there was a near collision or maybe a collision between me, on my 1983 Husky (Husqvarna 530cc dirt bike), and a couple of dirt bikes (motorcycle) on Spanish Mine Road. Alleghany is located on a ridge between the North and middle forks of the Yuba River. Washington is on the Yuba South fork. From Alleghany, I took Kanaka Road to Spanish Mine Road via Plumbago Road. Spanish Mine Road crosses Poorman's creek, then I hook up with the trail above Devil's canyon leading to Washington, about 20 miles. I had made the ride a number of times. It was in the evening, a beautiful high Sierra summer evening but still plenty of daylight. There had been a rain shower early that day and great traction. I was on a straight section of Spanish Mine Road that drops down a steep grade to Poorman's Creek, when without warning, two dirt bikes appeared, racing side by side up the road. There was nowhere to go. Hitting the brakes was not an option since that would cause a loss of control and almost guarantee a T-bone collision with me taking the blunt and surely badly injured. So, I twisted on the loud knob, pointed the Husky directly at the two damn fools and said to myself, "Okay, you're going to pay as much." I envisioned severe injury and worse but, in an instant, I was past them, cruising down the road. I did not have a clue how all the motorcycles avoided smashing into each other. Perhaps a twilight zone, maybe I'd landed in another world, universe, or something and was proceeding my life in another life cycle.

Be that as it may, my Husky was still vertical with the greasy side down, me on top in control. I drove the whole incident out of my mind and proceeded on my journey.

Poorman's creek needed to be crossed, not difficult but entertaining. The creek was running high, which made it a bit of a challenge, but I knew I could handle it. So as the saying goes, a journey starts with the first step. Me and my Husky plunged into the ice cold creek.

Poorman's Creek Crossing

As I approached the opposite bank out of the corner of my eye, I noticed a man standing to one side, looking at me. He was pretty rough looking, mid-thirties and dressed like a prospector. To my eyes, he looked like the real deal: dirt-soiled clothes, needing a shave and a bath. I had not noticed at first, but there was a mule behind him tied to a scrub oak. Upon clearing the creek, I pulled to one side, far enough to leave time for a quick escape, and then stopped. The man gave a slight salute and said, "That was

pretty interesting. You crossed the creek so quickly, and that is quite a machine you're riding. Do you have a name for that machine?"

"You mean this motorcycle? Have you been living under a rock or something," I replied sarcastically.

He look confused and said, "I did not mean to offend you young man, but I am not familiar with such a machine. At this point I had a familiar feeling, a déjà vu and said you are the slave pirate, Lynch. Christ, another journey into the past."

The man looked quite confused and said, "My name is Azriell Thomas Lynch and that's my mule, Princess. True, I was once such, but now I'm a prospector. We have been working in the area for a while, but no luck".

We, I said , don't see anybody but you here".

The old dude turned, looked at his mule and said "We, Princess and me".

So now, not sure if I, Bryan, made it through the collision. Maybe it was a hell of a collision, a front-page news accident, and I am in another universe, a different life cycle.

The old dude walked over to his mule and took a flask out from under the mule's pack. He opened it and took a swig while walking toward me and said, "This is a fine old Kentucky bourbon." He held it out and asked, "You'd like a swig? Must be cold after crossing the creek. This will warm the bones." After a pause and a moment to look me over, he said, "I have no idea where you come from and you are the first person I've seen all day, I've been working this creek for hours with no luck, I kind of feel we are both of another time, without a time compass, separated by a bit of time."

Well, I said, "Don't know anything about another time but I was on my way to the Washington Hotel just down the road a piece, that is, it always has been, and I sure hope it still is, whatever time we are in, I need something I can count on."

The old timer looking down at my riding boots said, "Those are some fancy boots, not good for walking, but seem to fit with the rest of your uniform. Are you a soldier?"

"No, but once I was a sailor, but now I am just a dirt bike rider needing a cold drink," and without another word mounted my Husky, slammed the kick starter down, twisted the loud knob, released the clutch and tore off in pursuit of a cold vodka and tonic.

Washington Hotel

It has a fine old bar with an old time feeling. The hotel sits on the South fork of the Yuba river, one of my favorite places. Not sure when it was constructed, but sometime in the 1850s. Hessel B. Buisman, I believe, owned it and Mr. Streeter from Graniteville was one of the principals. Anyway, that was my destination, Spanish Mine Road along the Devils Canyon to Gaston Road to Washington Road, to Washington Hotel. I love the old bar, the real deal, pretty much like it was back in the day.

The bar, a witness to a century of change, surge, and bust of the gold rush, winners and losers seeking gold and all its fringes, the loners searching for shelter from the demands of the industrial age, the occasional thirsty want-to-be somebody, dirt bike rider looking for a place to rest, like an old friend, a place you look forward to visiting.

The high Sierra night was approaching as the day gave way to the evening, a wonderful period of change. The old barroom seemed strangely pleasant and warm, but something seemed different. For one thing, everything looked newer; the mirror behind the bar was looking really good, like it had been replaced recently. Even the barkeep looked new, and surely younger than I expected. She was dressed in an old-fashioned outfit and very young, too young to be behind the bar. Be that as it may, I was going to order a drink; I said, "Young lady, I'd like a cold vodka and tonic."

She took a long, very long look at me, tilted her head slightly and said with a strong Spanish accent, "*Señor*, I do not know anything about vodka and tonic. We serve whiskey and beer. What would your pleasure be?"

I asked her name.

"Juanita," she replied with a not-just-another-yahoo look. She continued her busy work in an effort to conceal her distaste for another hit, just some stranger, a Joseph looking for refuge, shelter or maybe a little of that free love stuff.

Recognizing that look, I knew I had to change the subject because I was really only looking for a little conversation. I asked, "Have you seen an old prospector with a mule named Princess?"

"That seen to work, *Sí*, the confederate deserter?" she replied with a question.

Well, that did it, broke the ice. "Yes, ma'am, I just met him down by Poorman's Creek with his mule."

"You know, my dad was a confederate soldier," she said looking towards the doorway as the prospector wondered in, looking about, seemingly in dismay.

I thought, *She must have meant her grandfather, or else her father was a real old dude when he fathered her. She's quite young looking*. I thought of making a comment regarding the disparity, but thought better and said nothing.

Just about the time I was getting comfortable with the new Washington Bar look and the rather attractive young Hispanic lady the old timer peed over the low double door entrance and said "Well, young man, we meet again," looking at Juanita and speaking to me. "My name is Azriell Thomas Lynch, but I'm called Tommy." Then looking at me he asked, "Sir, how do I address you?"

"Bryan will work," I replied and added a question: "Where is your mule?"

"Oh, down at the livery station, unpacked and fed, she will be fine for the night. She needs a good night's rest. We are heading out tomorrow, heading north, want to prospect further north, not having much luck hereabout."

"Livery station," I said, looking at Juanita. "Hell, it's been many years since there's been a livery station here or any place with in a hundred miles." She looked at me with one of those 'Where have you been?' looks, and then at the prospector and said, "What's your order? The beer is cold, just took a half keg from the river."

Wow, now I know things have changed, I thought, no vodka tonic, no refrigeration, an old prospector, a young woman dressed in a 1800s outfit.

Juanita, looking at me but addressing the prospector, said, "Tell this man how you came by Princess, your mule."

"It was at the battle of Richmond, Kentucky, in Aug '62. We beat them Yankees at Richmond, Kentucky. The victory convinced a lot of Southerners they could win. It only convinced me that this war was going to be a long bloody struggle and to top it off, now I really did not want to die for the confederacy. Her death, Olivia, the sweet black slave seamstress, that beautiful young woman being held in slave bondage, was something I could no longer live with; not continue fighting for such a wrongful cause."

Olivia, who's Olivia, I thought, but I knew somehow, I knew that name, images of a young colored girl at the Glen Canyon campsite years ago flashed before me, I thought he was talking about her, but I did not want to interrupt him.

"During the battle, he continued still looking at Juanita, I happened upon a dying Yankee dressed in a strange looking uniform, dark blue jacket with red piping on the cuffs,". "The jacket was torn open and soaked in blood. A dark blue hunting-type cap laid nearby. There was a mule tied to a stump of a laurel tree. I figured it was his and he no longer needed that mule, and I could use it. It was not like I was stealing; I was just taking something he no longer needed. I had no idea how I could use a mule. Subconsciously, I think I had made a decision to escape, to desert, to get out of this dreadful war. He was lying nearby semi-conscious. He was about the age of my father, and I could not help but wonder how a man of his age did not know better than this. My first thought was to just leave him there to die, but he was clearly in pain and the best thing might be to simply end his agony, in a way as payment for the mule, with a clean shot to the head. As I aimed my rifle, he looked at me, fear, then hate, then acceptance in his eyes. He said, 'Well, young man, do what you must,' turned his head and waited for the shot.

"But an image of my pa flashed before my eyes, and I was compelled to stop and try to comfort him. I lowered my rifle, asked, 'Is there anything I can do?'

"He turned his head and looked at me. After a moment, I could see his focus cleared, but he said nothing. No idea where this came from. I said, 'Where are you from?'

"The question seemed to give him life. His eyes softened, and he said, 'You're about the age of a son, too young to be here. I am from New Port New Jersey; volunteered for the 44 New York. They said I was too long in the tooth, so I came to Tennessee, joined the Army of Ohio wearing my homemade uniform, my sister made it. Had to do something to save the union.'

"I said, looking at him, 'Old man, I'd think you would know better.'

"After what seemed like a long time, his eyes focused and after a long look, he replied, 'I be asking you the same. Gut shot and dying. Give me a drink of water, I'm terribly thirsty, then get me out of this misery. But first, I need to do one last good deed before answering for a life of misdeeds. My mule, Princess, is tied over there. Take care of her, she has some provisions, a flask of bourbon, a few greenbacks, take them and escape this ungodly war while you still can.'

"*Hell,* I thought, *Princess, a mule, who would name their mule Princess and I can just take that stuff; don't need to kill him to get them.* He turned his head, waiting for the shot, the passage to eternity. I started to walk away, could not, turned and fired, the shot was true, and his soul was free, free of worldly want, desire, pain, and disappointment."

"Oh," I interrupted the prospector and asked, "Was that flask of bourbon the one you offered me a swig of today the same flask? A stolen flask!"

The barkeep looked at the old dude and said, "Really, the same flask? I'd like a swig from it."

The want-to-be prospector, took a long look at her, asked, "What's your name, young lady? Are you the proprietor?"

She glanced at me, then a long appraising stare at Azriell Thomas Lynch, Juanita. "Who would want to be stuck here in this nowhere town? I want to go to the real city, San Francisco," was the reply.

He started laughing and said, "You are really an intrepid young lady, Juanita. You were born in the wrong century. I've been to San Francisco. I built a cabin there, young man, as Johnny, you lived there. But that's another story."

No Bryan, My Name is Bryan! I replied

"Well, you made a big deal about the slave pirate thing. You were Johnny when you resided in that cabin. The flask is in my pack in the stall next to my mule, but Princess is really protective, some other time, might be better. For now, I will gladly have the cold beer cooled from the river."

As Juanita poured him a beer, I said, "Yes, the cabin in the gold hills, but that is a different century and I have not been Johnny for years. Azriell Thomas Lynch, that's quite a name."

He took a swig of the beer and answered, more like his life story, occasionally looking at her to see if she was paying attention, how he had gotten into the confederate army and his family story. Why, I'm not sure, must have something to do with cycle, time, and some other stuff.

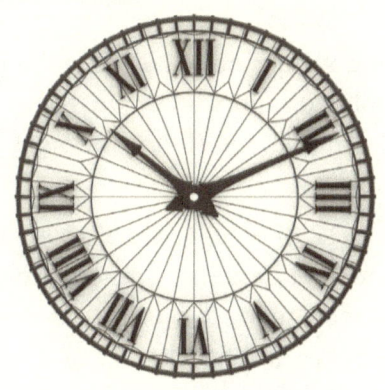

Chapter 11

Azriell Thomas Lynch

Lynch Family, 1860, Kentucky

The old prospector took another swig of beer, set down his mug and proceeded to tell us pretty much his life story. My family, he said, has lived in northern Kentucky, near the Ohio River, for as long as anyone can remember. Family lore has it that Great Granddad Lynch had fought with Morgan during the revolution back in 1783, that Great Grandpa Lynch settled into Kentucky when it was still Indian territory. We took pride in living on the same section of land for more than 50 years. Had paid for it in blood. The Charoke had no intention of giving up their land without a fight. Back in the early days during an Indian raid, G'G'dad lost two mules, a brother, and a leg and said he only missed the two mules, maybe the brother, too.

Our family's mantra is independence and self-sufficiency, do not need or want outside help. So, when the Yankees started shoving abolition down our throats, telling us what's right and wrong, we didn't take kindly to those outsiders butting into our business. We had no slaves, did not want them either, besides it was none of northern's business. The Lynch's believed, and it was confirmed by our church elders, our newspapers, our government leaders, that negroes were inferior, not equal to the white man and were better off being slaves than a freeman. As slaves, they were cared for and were productive. That, by nature, negroes were disorganized, undisciplined, and would run-a-muck as free men. How could the south deal with millions of loose cannons running loose in the countryside?

Like all my family, 12 of us, I have a biblical name, Azriell Thomas Lynch. I can read, write and speak in complete sentences when I choose to. Out there it's not smart to stand out, so I mostly talk like the locals, somewhere between Yankee and Southerner, and only as many words as necessary, a few words will do. They call me Tommy most of the time, unless my mom is mad, then it is 'you-no-good-for-nothing-boy'. I am the third youngest, two older brothers, Aaron and Adam.

Dad said, "Between the damn northern abolitionists, minding our business, and southern secessionists fools, there's going to be a war. It is not a smart war and is going to be bloody. All this nonsense about the northerners will not fight is hogwash. They're just as stubborn and tough and will fight. Pa said the older boys should go west and get clear of this mess and besides, it's time for them to be on their own, go west just like Great Granddad did, it's tough feeding 12 kids on this section of poor land."

I'll tell you about our plan; the three of us had a plan, we're going up to Ohio to capture a nigger, and sell him to Colonel Gilmore for $300, that's a lot of money for a slave but the Colonel has one negro in mind, that negro they call 'the Educated Nigger Farmer' across the river in Ohio. Well, anyway, we were going to use the money to go to California.

You know I don't see anything wrong with being educated, we're sometimes called those 'educated white trash', cause dad insisted on all his kids reading. He'd said, "Just because we're poor, we don't need to be uneducated." Miss Elinor, our neighbor, the old maid from back East, taught us to read, write and other stuff like history.

Aaron changed the plan, he said, "The slave market in New Orleans is paying $500. We can sell the nigger there and book passage to California with the extra $200." He'd heard anyone can strike it rich. Gold is everywhere in the mountains. All you need is determination and a shovel.

I told Aaron, "Pa said I could not go on the raid with them. I was too young and you two could handle it by yourselves."

Aaron said they needed three people because they had to keep watch on the negro all the way to New Orleans, a three-day trip and to heck with Pa. "I've been told that negro has a farm just across the Ohio River just off the River Road. If we leave early in the morning, we can be there by tomorrow morning. Are you coming?"

So off we went to catch a slave and seek our fortunes, three young men, two donkeys, one well-used musket and dreams of glory. Little did we know we were heading directly into harm's way, but that's another story.

"Oh yes," he said, looking at me, "That's right. Theodore told you about that, how the rebels confiscated the slaves and forced us to join the Army of Tennessee."

Wholly cow, I thought, *he knows I've met Theodore, How? This cycle in cycle stuff, I suppose!*

Juanita, puzzled, asked, "Who is Theodore?"

Looking at her, he said, "The Educated Negro, Theodore Washington Jones, one of the slaves we captured, we were on the way to the slave market when a rebel platoon confiscated the slaves and inducted us into the army," he answered.

Well, here I, Azriell Thomas Lynch was as much a captive as our Going-to-California-Ticket slaves. No uniform, no training, no clue, but I'm in the army. A Confederate soldier, just a kid heading in to battle, or maybe kingdom come. The scuttlebutt has it we got to kick those Yankees out of some camp up north, years later I was told it was Camp Wildcat, the Battle of Camp Wildcat. Aaron and Adam were somewhere attacking the union army and I'm waiting my turn, a kid or not.

The Boss Sergeant said the Yankees at Camp Wildcat are putting up a hell of a fight and all able men are needed. He handed me a flintlock rifle and ordered me to join a group of tobacco spitting men.

Man, the next thing, I'll be charging a parapet filled with Yanks aiming to kill me, I thought. Then I noticed a bunch of soldiers in total disorder running toward us shouting, "Yanks have breached! Get the hell out of here"; the tobacco spitting men stopped spitting, They looked at each other and started running, where, no one knows just as long as it is opposite to the sounds of fighting. For just a moment, I just stood there looking around as the Yankees charged uphill, directly toward me. I dropped to one knee and pulled the trigger.

Bang, this antique rifle went off, smoke and all. A charging Yankee went down in a heap. The wave of charging blue soldiers stalled for a moment. The Boss Sergeant fired and then the few remaining soldiers started firing. The charging Yankees stopped running, dropping to the ground, and began firing at us. I could hear the bullets whistling past. A soldier a few feet away moaned in pain and fell face down into the muddy Kentucky ground. The Boss Sergeant ordered us to withdraw. Like trained men, my fellow soldiers began drifting back, kneeling, and firing in an orderly manner. The Yankees held their position long enough to allow us to retreat from the field of battle. The battle, my first, was over. I felt a surge of feelings, pride, fear, relief, and something new, a feeling of being a man, a warrior.

I began searching for my brothers, Aaron and Adam, the last I'd heard they were on the parapet with some of the Tennessee soldiers but after the Yankees bridged our line and the retreat started, no one seemed to know or care about their whereabouts. Hell, I might be a warrior, but I missed my brothers. We had started out for California, ended up in the rebel army, at least I did. I had no clue as to the whereabouts of my brothers. Maybe they had deserted or, worse yet, dead.

It was getting late; the sun was almost gone, the cool wind blowing through the Columbian Gap was chilling my bones, I was tired and alone. I joined a few soldiers sitting around a campfire, trying to ward off the cold October night air and the feeling of defeat.

So, Bryan, here's how I became an officer, a Brevet Lieutenant in the Confederate army; Boss Sergeant, accompanied by an officer, approached us. I had not seen many officers since I volunteered, more like appropriated a few months ago, but this one looked grand in his fine gray and blue uniform.

The sergeant pointed towards me, and the officer said, "Young man, you were magnificent today. I want to commend you for your courage under fire and have recommended a promotion to Brevet Lieutenant. We need officers that will stand their ground and control their men. I will see to it that you will be issued a uniform and receive the appropriate pay. Welcome aboard. We have a tough road ahead of us, but I assure you the Confederate States will prevail, and its citizens will enjoy real freedom." The officer then addressed the Boss Sergeant, "Sergeant, you bring this young man by the headquarters tomorrow. I will have it arranged to make him a proper uniform."

"Yes, sir," he replied as the two of them turned and walked away.

They were hardly out of earshot when a soldier sitting across the campfire asked, "Do you know who that was?"

"No," I answered.

"That was General Zollicoffer, one of the richest men in Kentucky." After a long appraisal of me, he said, "What in the hell did you do to rate this?"

One of the other soldiers said, "He was the soldier who rallied the troops after the union broke through our line down at the Wildcat Battle."

Then another chipped in, "All we need is another know-nothing kid officer."

Well, that is his opinion, but I figured I earned it because I am a warrior and I intend to fulfill my obligation to my country, the Confederate States of America.

Little did I know, but Brevet means temporary, just a wartime thing. It was not long before I knew he had no intention of giving me any real authority. Using me to promote the ideal of 'stay your position', be obedient and you will be rewarded. I learned to respect Zollicoffer. The General was opposed to the war, had been a Tennessee State Senator, a delegate to the peace conference, against Tennessee secession, but here he was leading an army against the Union. And here I am, 'the big warrior', putting myself in harm's way because of a number of errors and mistakes.

Within a few months, the term 'harm's way' took on a real meaning. All that being said, I had lucked out. As an officer I got a officer's, uniform, the one Olivia made for me and I was allowed to bunk in the general's headquarters, way better than the soldier's makeshift camp. The headquarters had real tents, not lean-to canvas.

Juanita interrupted the prospector with a question, "Olivia, what was the deal with her? Tell me about her?"

Azriell Thomas Lynch, stopped talking, took a very long look at Juanita, as if the question had invoked a painful memory and started talking about another subject:

While I grew up in a slave state, I had very little contact with any slaves, except for the Educated Negro Farmer and that did not turn out well. Pa considered that slave stuff as unholy and he was an abolitionist at heart. I had thought that slaves were mainly used for harvesting crops, field workers. Oh, I'd heard of the house negro. I understood they were like the chosen-ones, smart and appealing in appearance. I had no idea they could be a tailor.

Hell, I wore hand-me-down homemade clothes. As promised, the General arranged for a uniform and sent me to his tailor in Logan's Crossroads. I expected the tailor to be some man, working out of a small shop somewhere in town. The owner of the shop was an older man with an Irish accent and a preference for distilled beverages. You could tell by the red nose, bad breath, and shaky hands. He greeted me and said, "Well, young man, what can I do for you?"

"General Zollicoffer has ordered a uniform for me at your shop."

"Yes, I remember, an officer's," he replied and then added, "Beat the hell out of those Yankee bastards." He turned and called out, "Olivia, we have a customer." A young negro slave girl came into the room. I guess she was 13 or 14. "Olivia, this young man is here for the uniform ordered by the general. Take care of him."

So, his young negro seamstress is the tailor. She seemed way too young to be so skilled. I was told he purchased her from a local plantation owner after hearing about her sewing skills, but as I learned years later, they were related through his cousin, and he was kind of fathering her.

As Olivia entered the room, she was carefully looking down, keeping her eyes downcast, never meeting my eyes and only spoke when spoken to. She used the 'Yes-um, no sir, and don't know' when she avoided answering. But there was something special about her. Besides being pleasing to look at, she carried herself with dignity. But then our eyes met just for a moment, when she dared to stay, fixed for what seemed forever, then she looked away. My knees felt like they might buckle. I was astonished. This was something new to me. In all my 15 years, I had never experienced this, and it scared me.

She made a fine uniform in the classic confederate gray and blue and in the process of measuring, cutting and trying I fell in love with her, but the affair was one-sided. She skillfully avoided any sign of acknowledging it, diligently performing the tailoring task. Be that as it may, I could not forget or help wanting her. I was looking for an opportunity to impress her and possibly turn her head, her feeling, affection toward me.

A few weeks later, my squad was ordered into the nearby town of Somerset to pick up supplies, coffee, sugar, and beans. Hell, the Boss Sergeant said, "We might as well stop by Somerset Way Station on the way back and get some of that fine Kentucky Whiskey."

Now, we had a few green back dollars in our pocket to spend, and we didn't know if we'd live long enough to spend it somewhere else. We got paid in the new graybacks, confederate dollars, but no one seemed to accept them.

After the supplies were loaded, couldn't get much coffee, damn Yankee blockade, but a lot of sugar and beans, on the return trip we just happened to pass the Somerset Way Station, a converted barn on Old Road, and since we had a few green back not needed for the coffee, I decided to purchase some fine Kentucky bourbon for our supplies. As it turned out, Roberts, the proprietor, was so happy to get greenbacks he offered us a little free bourbon. By chance, the old Irish tailor was there indulging in his favorite beverage.

After a moment, the Irish tailor recognized me and said, "You're that fine young confederate officer that is going to beat the hell out of those bastard Yankees. Let me buy you and the soldiers a drink and give you some information."

"First, the drinks, then the information," the Boss Sergeant said.

Well, with a couple shots of Kentucky bourbon under my belt and information that the Educated Negro Farmer was in Logan's Crossroads being fitted, I decided that there was a chance to capture a couple of

Yankee soldiers and an escaped negro slave and see Olivia. But I knew, come what may, I could not let on that I favored the negro seamstress.

So, feeling a little like a Napoleon in training, I ordered my squad to proceed to Logan's Crossroads to capture the Yankees, and the escaped slave. At first, the men were taken back by my order, but when the Boss Sergeant backed me, we were off like a band of thieves in pursuit of treasure.

The caper, my big plan to capture a couple of Yankee soldiers, an escaped slave and be a hero, went really bad, damn near losing a wagon, supplies, two mules, and my life. To top it off, I made a fool of myself, and Olivia must have thought I'm a real jerk.

"Hell, we were damn near captured by some Yanks and I thought I might have killed Olivia, just got out with the supplies but I don't want to talk about it."

Juanita asked, "Is that when you decided to desert?"

"Not sure," he replied, "but I was thinking about it and after I acquired the mule, I guess I knew I was going to get out of this war somehow."

A couple of weeks later, I was all set. I was deserting. I had Princess, my newly acquired mule, packed and ready to go, was startled by the sudden approach of a man. It was the Boss Sergeant, and I thought, *Oh, hell what now?*

I said in my best officer's tone, "Sergeant, you performed excellently the other day and were an important factor in our success."

He just looked at me for a moment and replied, "Cut the horseshit. You're no real officer and I did not contribute a damn thing. I was lucky not to be dead." He then took a long careful look at the mule and said, "You're heading out tonight; what's your plan?"

I thought I was caught. How in the hell did the Boss know?

The Sergeant asked, "Boy, do you think I am stupid or just dumb? Ever since that black girl was killed, you've been looking for a way out. Shit, everyone can see you are going to desert, given the chance."

"Okay Sergeant, I am leaving tonight, heading for St. Louis, intend to hitch up with one of those wagon trains going to California. Figure tonight during the late-night watch. The posted men are often asleep."

Sergeant looked at Princess, said, "Not smart, you'll get shot, hell the guard will think you are Union, they are real nervous with Sheridan in the area. Best we leave during chow time this evening, just walk out like we got an assignment, have to travel at night through confederate territory to Paducah, it is under Union control. Just hope we don't get shot. Need to ditch these uniforms, get some civilian outfits. I am going with you."

Well, you know Bryan; the Sarge and me were real lucky we just walked out of the camp like we had orders, travel through the confederate's defensive perimeter through the night without a hitch. In the morning we ditched our uniforms, had civilian out fit in Princes's packing, and the three of us hitched a ride on a river boat to St. Louis. I think the mule gave us the appearance of farmers going to the market. We were heading for California but had to make a detour through Montana Territory.

We should have gone to California, hell it was Boss Sergeant's fault. He heard it was better picking in Montana Territory. I wanted to go to California and a party looking to hire help was leaving for California on Tuesday morning, but the steamboat with supplies from Gilbert's point was delayed due to rebel activity. This was unfortunate for me and the Boss Sergeant because it delayed our departure; we were in a hurry to get out of the area quickly. Three rebel deserters, well Princess have no choice and she probably was thinking speak for yourself I am a Yankee..

The Sergeant heard of another wagon train; it had left a week earlier, bogged down at a creek crossing, a day's ride and they could use some help, but it was in route to Montana Territory, and he felt it was destiny and better anyway.

Hell, Bryan, he said looking down at his half empty beer mug, if the Montana diversion was destiny it must have been a pay-back-destiny for a couple of misfit deserters.

Bryan, the winters there would make believers out of you, would convert to any religion if you thought it would help you stay alive. So, we were somewhere in the territory. It was midafternoon, the northern bitterroot wind was blowing in gusts, each gust blew clouds of snow and seemed colder than the last. I sat on a stump as close to the fire as possible, thinking, *Doesn't winter end in Montana Territory?*

You know, the prospector said looking at the young bar maid, our stay in Montana was rather short. I will relate the details of the event that triggered a hasty departure. So, here we were, Boss Sargent, Princess, and I, freezing cold somewhere in Montana Territory. Princess was uneasy, she'd been for a while. By the flickering firelight, I could just make out a man's silhouette standing not more than a few yards away. I was so startled, I just froze. He seemed to notice my reaction, fear, surprise, concern, and said: *"Parlez-vous francais?"*

I did not answer; I understood the question, had heard enough French to understand. He cautiously approached. He was a big man, wearing a heavy buffalo hide coat and a strange-looking fur hat. He stood near the fire opposite me for a few moments without speaking; then said, "My name is Louis. I am a priest from St Peter's Mission. I lost my way in the storm and perhaps faith brought me to your fire."

I could just make out a brown robe under his coat. I had heard about Jesuit priests, the soldiers of God but did not expect one to be out here in the middle of the night, must be ten below.

After recovering from the shock, I replied, "No, do you speak English?"

"Yes," he replied with a German accent. This made me uneasy. He was not French; then why did he ask me if I could speak French? He then said, "I am not French, no longer a priest, lost my faith in the church but not in the holy trinity, gave up the cloth, just a prospector now." He took a step closer, looking around the camp, then at me, I had the feeling he was measuring, appraising, evaluating, checking to see if I was alone. For the first time, I noticed the Sergeant was not there. He must have moved out of the firelight.

The ex-priest, still sizing the situation, asked, "Are you all alone?"

I did not reply.

"Any luck prospecting?"

I did not answer.

Then a couple of people, a woman in an Indian blanket which covered her head and then a young man, maybe a boy, stepped into the firelight. The young man was wearing a union army winter coat and hat. You could see he was not European, maybe a half-breed. They were in bad shape, desperate.

The woman and young man walked directly past me, began cutting, bending small aspen trees. After a number of trees, enough to serve as a windbreak, they packed it with snow. Satisfied with their work, they made a small fire within the protected area, sat down, huddled near the fire. The ex-priest, Louis, saw the confusion in my eyes and said, "Indians make small fires and sit close, white men make a large fire and sit far away. Come sit with them," and pointed towards the woman, "Alona and her son. Get warm, you will see their way is better. Alona is Hebrew and means 'oak tree' I call her that because she is tall, stands straight, and is beautiful."

I had to agree, even in the dimly flicking firelight I could see her fine facial features. Be it native, it was still handsome.

Boss Sargent stepped out of the shadows and in French began to recite a Psalm, *"Quand je marche dans la vallée de l'ombre de la mort, Je ne crains aucun mal, car tu es avec moi: Ta houlette et ton bâton me rassurent."*

I almost knew it by heart because he gave it a number of times on the battlefield. I asked him where he'd learned it, but he always just clammed up and gave the 'do not ask again' look. The ex-priest started laughing but the laugh quickly turned to moans, then to crying, stopped crying, softly repeated in English, "Yea, though I walk through the valley of the shadow of death, I will fear no evil: for thou art with me; thy rod and thy staff, they comfort me. Thou preparest a table before me in the presence of my enemies: thou anointest my head with oil; my cup runneth over."

"I need to make a confession, the ex priest said looking at the small fire, to cleanse my soul before I must answer to my lord. Then looking at Sarge he said "You, my killer, my dispatcher, must be my priest, my connection to Jesus." The Sarge looked at me and I am sure he was thinking, 'I wish I had not started with the religious stuff.'

Louis removed a Remington 1851 revolver, the same type of revolver issued to Union officers, from under his coat, flipped it handle first, extended his arm and looked at me and said, "You are a soldier and I beg of you dispatch this wretched soul; for I have violated god's commandment. Exodus 20:2-17 thou shalt not kill; thou shalt not covet another man's wife,"

Stunned, I did not know what to do or what to make of it; I stood there in a daze. Sarge walked over, took the revolver, and said, "This is a 1851 Navy revolver. How did you come by it?" Now, Louis looked bewildered.

Then staring at the defrocked priest, Sarge said, "We were soldiers not executioners."

I said, "Covet another man's wife, not a reason to kill yourself. I think if that was so, all males are guilty, and I know damn well I am."

Boss Sergeant nodded his head in agreement. And said, "Ya brother."

Louis, not looking at us, said, "Yes, but I covet not just a man's wife but the holy trinity's, a nun at the mission. For you see, nuns are married to God. they live under vow of chastity, and I seduced her, a sister, God's wife and slept with her."

Sarge tried handing the revolver back to the priest and said, "If you are in so much pain, then use the gun on yourself and end it."

Louis would not take it, waved his hand in the air and said "It is a mortal sin to take your own life, I will let mother nature do it, so I bid you *adieu* with one last request, protect Alona and her son until you have reached a safe place, she has endured so much pain and suffering, it is the least we Europeans can do."

Alona and her son sat quietly under the aspen tree shelter, staring at the fire as Louis made a slight bow turn and proceeded to leave the camp in a northern direction. Sarge looked at Alona, then at me and said, "I think that is not the last of him. Be on guard. Watch your mules and supplies. We will need them more now that we have two more to feed."

Alona looked up and for the first time spoke, in French, which Sarge, translated, "Come sit by the fire, warm yourself and I will sing."

Well, I thought that was a good idea. My hands were freezing, and my feet felt frozen, and besides, I always like being with women.

After a spell, Alona began to hum, softly at first, then louder with a rhythm. It was rather peaceful, and I started to drift off to sleep, but Sarge shook me and said, "Stay awake and keep your wits about." Sarg looked at me and whispered, "Watch the woman and the boy, I will look for that priest." I guess Sarge was not taking any of Louis's bullshit and figured he had already sold his soul to Satan, that the young man was not her son, that all three of them were thieves about to bushwhack us.

Sarge was not gone but a few minutes and I heard a nearby shot, maybe 100 yards to my left somewhere in the trees, then the young man stood up and pointed a revolver at me but almost in the same instant, Alona whacked him in the knees with a branch or something, causing his shot to miss me. Another shot from the dark. The young man groaned, pitched forward, and fell into the fire. Alona jumped up and ran out of camp and disappeared into the woods.

I was totally confused at that point. The young man did not move. His body was smothering the fire, and I was alone in the dark. I saw figure emerging out of the darkness, I thought of following Alona and running for my life, but then it was Sarge and he told me to "Stay where you are, I will check out the boy."

After Sarge rolled him over and pulled him out of the fire, it burst into flames. Sarge asked, "Where is the woman?"

Dumbfounded, I replied, "Don't know." I pointed into the woods, "She ran like a bat-out-of-hell in that direction."

Sarge said, looking in the direction I was pointing, "She was one beautiful woman. We'll pack up in the morning and head out, we need to put some distance between us and these dead men, don't want to try to explain shooting a boy and priest, they tend to make quick judgements and dispense justice real quick in the territory. We will head due south for California."

At that point both Juanita and I were pretty tired of this story and I am sure she have more important things todo , or may be just wished this old dude would shut up but I said, "Tommy, this was a hell of a story but I have a rather long ride ahead of me, getting late, got to cross a creek, I'm going to say goodbye and wish you and Princess the best of luck in your prospecting venture."

I took one last look at Juanita, grabbed my riding gear, thought to myself, *Got to get out of here while the getting is good.*

I'm not sure if I, Bryan, made it through the collision. Maybe it was a hell of a collision, a front-page news accident, and I am in another century, universe, life cycle. No vodka tonics, not sure I was in the right place or time, could see some daylight still shining through the doors and figured there was still time enough for a return trip.

I said my goodbyes, put on my helmet, my gloves, tightened my kidney belt, mounted my bike, slammed down the kick starter, rode my Husky back the way I came, hoping things will be real, present not the past. I proceeded to use my loud knob liberally, tracing my route back to Downieville. Poorman's Creek was colder and deeper and the whole return trip seem twice as long.

Sure enough, thank God, Downieville looked the same, a welcome sight. I cruised down Gallaway's Grade past the hangmen's noose, across the Yuba river bridge, into my night's lodging parking area. My dark green 1969 Camaro, California license, 1973 bright orange yearly license tabs, bike trailer and all was parked in the Downieville Motor Lodge parking lot: Alright, things are normal, maybe I'll just treat this day as a dream, not too good a dream, no vodka tonic. I thought about that attractive young Hispanic bar keep, Juanita and the Juanita of the eighteen hundred hanging. A coincidence?

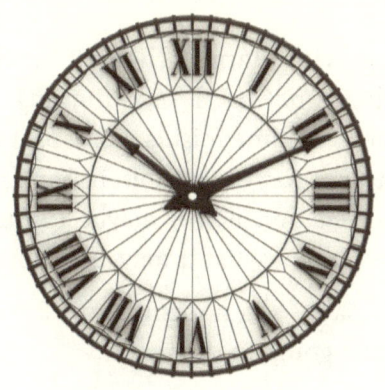

Chapter 12

Another Meeting

A Real Estate investor

Back in the day, that is in the 1850s , soon after the Yankees confiscated Alta California from the Mexicans, Yerba Buena Cove was renamed San Francisco. Jasper O'Farrell laid out a new city street grid. Blackstone Court, a street built on an early trail that ran from town toward the Presidio around the north end of Washerwoman's Lagoon, a street diagonal to Jasper O'Farrell's grid, can be found if one wants, near the old Washerwoman's lagoon. I love those things, an error resulting in something out of order but neat. Across the street, Franklin St, there was a grocery store, a fine old Italian grocery store with baccala, dried salted cod, filled the air with an unmistakable aroma, which defined the store as a real Italian store. I'd often stop there, not sure why, but they had Italian style ice cream, great vanilla. I'd buy a cone and meander across Franklin to visit a small section of the past.

Allowing my mind to drift back in time, envisioning Blackstone Ct. of the past. I realized that my trips to the past occur in an area with a past, a past that is still present. There was a cleaned up, shaved, newly attired Azriell Thomas Lynch. As I looked, I recognized him. He must have read my mind, he said, "Bryan, my friends call me Tommy."

Another meeting with Azriell Thomas Lynch: *Christ, why me,* I thought, what is about me that I keep running into these long, but seemingly not forgotten rag-time misfits, perhaps it has something to do with the long gone but not forgotten cabin in San Francisco's gold hill or maybe I am just a clueless dreamer or maybe I insulted some deity and now it is getting even, be that what it may, here goes.

"Well, Tommy," I said, "I'm not going to ask you how, why or when you got here, so I'm just going to go with it."

He replied, "I'd be asking you the same."

I asked "Tommy, still prospecting?"

"No, I am a businessman now, in real estate. I made some money up in Dawson City, in Alaska, stash it at Well Forgo. There is some property here in the old Spanish section I am considering."

"I wish you the best of luck, Azriell Thomas Lynch, in your new venture, but I've been thinking about the last time we met, you were prospecting in the South fork of the Yuba River. Where's Princess, your mule?"

"She passed a while ago," he replied. "After Princess passed, she must have been bitten by a rattler or ate a poison mushroom, can't tell for sure but she just would not get up one morning and was gone by night, I drifted down to Sacramento, met a young man with lots of money, said he'd struck it near bear creek south of Dawson, sold me a map. The map was just a scam, no good, should have known better. Guess it was payback for the gold mine scam thing me and Sarge pull off a few years ago. But I did well, hit some pay dirt, traded it for a riverboat, made a lot of money ferrying goods on the Yukon River. Decided to invest it into city real estate as TW Jones did. It seems strange how the three of us, Olivia, Theodore, and I ended up here in San Francisco, must be fate, that is the only way. You know Olivia changed her name. She is now Mary Kelly, a white woman. But be that as it may, she's still beautiful, and I am interested in her black or white.

"Have I ever told you about my desertion from the confederate army?" He continued.

"Tommy, I've heard that story, I said, the Washington Hotel, remember? It had something to do with a young negro girl. Tell me about San Francisco's gold mine scam and building that cabin?"

Yes, he said as he lunched in to a rather long story; That cabin in the San Francisco hills, it was back in the 70s. We, Boss Sergeant and me, after a hasty departure from Montana, were in need for some cash, ran into a fellow in a bar downtown that was working on a scam, a salted mine with phony stocks, needed someone to dig it and build a cabin. Needed money, took the job. So, to the hills we went, the three of us, me, boss sergeant and Princess, to earn some cash.

I remember the Sergeant asking, "Are you sure that guy owns this section? We can dig a mine here? Do you think that worthless scrounge mule of yours can haul the mine material up this hill?"

"Yes, sir," I told him mockingly. "Louis Alfred Pioche purchased it from the Horner brothers who bought it from Noé himself and "Pioche arranged to buy and have the material brought here". I heard a few years later he sold most of the property to another guy, a money guy, Mr. TW Jones. I heard he made a lot of money in the real estate business. I remember telling Princess how I like the weather in California, a hell of a lot better than Montana but this Frisco fog can get under your skin," Boss Sergeant added as he padded her rump, "Tell that nitwit, it's San Francisco not Frisco, you know the locals call it San Francisco and we want people to think we're legitimate local businessmen."

"Yes," Boss Sergeant said as he kicked a small rock and looked at Princess and the rocky hillside. "I hope this works, this gold mine scam, cause this rocky hill property is not good for nothing else. Are we going to camp around here?" Looking at me, he said, "Mr. TW Jones sounds familiar. Remember that educated negro you and your brothers were taking to the slave market, what was his name?"

"Yes, I remember. You and a bunch of rebels screwed up our big plan and his name was Theodore Washington Jones," I replied. "Everyone called him the Educated Negro Farmer, but hell, we're in California, 2000 miles away, no way, it can't be. He was probably killed during the war."

"Okay, I think you're right," Boss Sergeant said, changing the subject. "We should construct the cabin first, then go about digging the mine."

I said as I pointed up the hill, "Up there about 100 yards is an old campsite, great view of the canyon and a spring nearby."

Boss Sergeant thought about it for a moment then said, "It's getting late, the morning around here can get really cold with the fog, let's start setting up the camp before it gets dark."

That cabin functioned as a mine office, part of the gold mine scam. Little by little, the cabin became our residence. At Louis' expense, we added a potbelly stove and outhouse. For nearly 2 years, while the scam played out, the cabin became a place to live, but then, like all illegal scams, word got out. I realized Mr. Pioche had set us up as the fall guys; his story was, he, Louis Alfred Pioche, was just an honest businessman who had been duped by those two dishonored ex-rebel soldiers.

Given our predicament, we decided the best course was to hightail it out of San Francisco before some volunteer justice committees caught up with us; the committees handed out serious and expeditious justice. I felt I still had wild oats to sow and new places to see. I headed for the hills, Sierra gold country. Sergeant said he was going to search for Alona and then returned to Tennessee since the war was now more or less relegated to the past. The South was busy rebuilding and there was an opportunity to make money.

Tommy stopped talking for moment, looked at the ice cream I was holding, I realized my Italian vanilla ice cream was melting, I had been so engrossed in Tommy's account of the gold hill scam I had forgotten it and now I had a decision, stay and try to save it which required devour it at a high rate or excuse myself and find a trash can, I chose to excuse myself, I was a little nervous about the whole thing, a hundred year old story being related in a street of the past, so I said " Tommy, it was delightful seeing you again, that was a interesting story but I have to dump this ice cream before it melts all over my hand.

He looked dumbfounded and said "shit just dump it on the street". That remark brought home the fact that our life cycles where separate by a hundred odd years besides it was a poor excuse anyway and I did not try to justify it but simply said " Until we meet again don't take any wooden nickels or buy any worthless gold mine maps and then proceeded to find my car before it disappeared in to some kind of time sink hole.

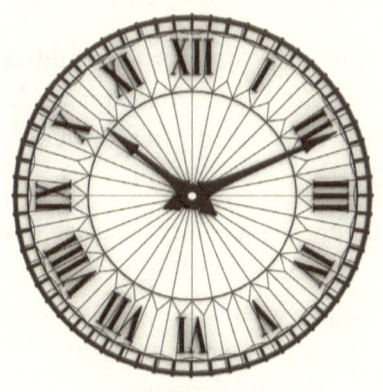

Chapter 13

Becoming TW Jone

A Businessman

There's an area in San Francisco known as Barbary Coast. It is not much more than a tourist trap now, but in the day it was a pretty wild place and if you look carefully and you are lucky, you can still spot some of its old glory. Well, I know it will sound like I spent a lot of time in bars, and I confess I have a weak spot for old ones. I'm not sure why, but perhaps I can feel the past, thinly veiled by the present. If you know old San Francisco, there's a narrow alley off Columbus with my kind of bar and if you are lucky, it is mostly empty of tourists. When I get a longing for the past, it is one of my stops. If it is a slow night, the barkeep would allow me to smoke my cigar in the corner near a small, well abused window. This area has a venerable small tavern table that had seen better days, with a couple of well used but comfortable high-back chairs. It was a bit from the bar, and I could pass the time doing my favorite thing, observing people doing their thing. I sat in the chair near the window with my back to the wall, smoking my Arturo Fuente Hemingway, drinking neat Jamison and observing a couple of sailors in a serious discussion about the best bar in town.

The 1950-style Wurlitzer Jukebox was playing Johnny Ace's *Pledging My Love*, sounded like the old days, music that can't be found in a run of a mill gin-mill. I was really comfortable and began thinking about some of the places I'd been as a sailor, bars, places, like Blackmarket Alley Yokosuka, Japan. Bars were named after the US battleships, Missouri, Iowa and so on.

I was deep in memories, a Black Market bar of my youth when I realized there was somebody standing behind the chair opposite me. That startled me back to here and now. A man, a well-dressed African American, three-piece suit, gray vest, black bow tie, gold pocket watch chain and all looked like he'd just stepped out of the gay nineties, that's the 1890s and said with a smile, "Bryan, I figured I would meet you again in some dive. But I did not want to alarm you. You looked as if you were somewhere pleasant."

At first, I thought, *Oh, God my past is catching up with me,* then I recognized him, and thought, *Yes, it has.*

I thought—or maybe hoped—the Theodore Washington Jones thing was a dream, a figment of imagination, the past, but here he was standing in front of me.

"Oh Bryan, you thought you'd seen the last of me; the last time I saw you, you were soaking wet wearing a garbage bag and riding gear. In Alleghany, the little town in the Sierras, do you remember? It seems our cycle has commingled again, maybe because I frequented this bar back when the Barbary Coast was in its prime. Do you mind me sitting here and join you? I enjoy talking with you, one of the special people, and tell you about a very little battle at Logan's Crossroads, how I joined the Union army and my move to California," he said as he took the chair opposite me without waiting for a reply.

That will be swell Theodore , or should I address you a T W Jones?, and why do want to tell me this story? I asked

Ignoring the questions he began with his story. After the Union victory at Camp Wildcat and my escape from rebels, I, Theodore Washington Jones, stayed with Portsmouth Militia and did whatever I could to defeat my enemy, my would-be slave owners. In the meantime, I wanted to get out of the rags I was wearing, but I had little opportunity to acquire anything new, so I washed up my ragged clothes the best I could. Then, on the third day of my newfound freedom, the Neighbor,

Lieutenant Ludwick, surprised me with a gift of new clothes, a tailored set. He said he'd taken up a collection among the troops and many of them contributed. He said they agreed I should have civilian, not army dress. One of the local boys, Private Jefferson, knew of a tailor at Logan's Crossroads. It was arranged to have two soldiers accompany me to the shop for my protection.

The shop owner, an older Irishman with the smell of whisky on his breath, greeted us and said, "This is the educated negro farmer I've heard about."

Does everyone know about me? I thought.

Then he said, "You Yankee boys need to beat the hell out of the no-account rebels." He then loudly called out, "Olivia!" and a young colored girl entered the room. He looked at me and said, "She is the seamstress that will make your new outfit."

Olivia took a second look. She must have thought, *the first black man I ever had as a customer and he's in rags, is this some kind of joke?*

I saw a confusion in her eyes and said in perfect English with a slight southern accent added just for the effect, "Young lady, this attire is only temporary. Once I am appropriately dressed, you will behold the real me." Then I added after a short delay, "I clean up real good."

I could see Olivia was confused and must have thought *who is this colored man? He talks like a white man. He cannot be a free negro cause they would not dress like that, a slave.*

One of the soldiers understood the confusion and said, "This is Theodore Washington Jones, the Educated Negro Farmer from Ohio and now an adjutant in the Army of Mississippi. He needs a new set of clothes."

Olivia took another long look at me and said, "I don't know nothing about some educated negro farmer from Ohio, but I will be pleased to make this man a new set of clothes. But first he needs a bath. Just down the street is a boarding house where he can get a bath and clean up. After he is cleaned up, bring him back and I'll make measurements and fit him next week."

The soldier looked at her and said, "That will not do, we will be gone by then. He needs to be fitted today."

The owner stepped in and said, "Well, that will be double the price."

Then, Private Jefferson, the local boy, with a glare said, "It will be done at original price and by tonight else I'll run you in for supplying comfort to the enemy, everyone knows you are playing both sides of the street."

After a moment, the Irish owner said, "Yes, sir, it will be ready."

It was already getting dark by the time Olivia entered the room with my new clothes. As she handed me the outfit, I noticed a small piece of paper neatly tucked in the folds of the trousers. I looked at her; she glanced at the paper and looked into my eyes and quickly walked out. It was clear to me it was a warning, and that Olivia was risking her life in passing it on. I took the clothing directly behind the privacy screen without acknowledging the note.

Out of sight and behind the screen, I immediately read it: *'Your life's in danger. You must not take Somerset Road east, ambush at the old road, go west to the boarding house, cut through the pasture, bypass the junction of old road and Somerset.'*

I have to tell you that the seamstress had made an impression on me. Once she dropped the slave act, it was clear she felt and acted as a free person, smart and articulate. She seemed particularly warm toward me; she made unnecessary but welcomed eye contact. But the last thing I need right now is another person, especially a loved one, to care for. Hell, I had a bloody fight ahead and, most likely, a short life.

The suit fit fine and felt great, I felt like a whole man again, free from the humiliating feeling of being a slave. The feeling would last a lifetime. One of the soldiers, the local kid, said he felt something was going on and wanted to take a look before I left the building. I told him about the note and he and the other trooper decided to bushwhack those rebels at the stable.

Olivia led the trooper and me to the door, but indicated we should hesitate as she opened and looked about. She nodded her head, looking at the soldier, and he proceeded through the doorway. She then did something surprising. She held my hand for a long moment as she looked into my eyes; I felt as if she could see all of me, past, present, and future. Strange how a moment can seem like an eternity.

Our horses were in the livery stable just down the road a short bit. The soldier nudged me as he noticed a wagon across the road; it seemed to be loaded with two Tennessee mules still harnessed. Very suspicious. A couple of men stood up behind it and said, "Put down your arms, you are under arrest and a prisoner of the Army of Tennessee."

"Under arrest, what the hell are you jabbering about?"

The soldier said, "I know you, you're that Lynch boy. What are you doing in that rebel uniform, anyway? I heard you were on your way to California."

A Union Soldier, the other escort, stepped out from behind the stable doors and shouted, "No, you damn fools, put down your weapons. You are under arrest by the Army of Mississippi."

A few chaotic shots were fired by the soldiers; the two Tennessee mules jolted, started running, still attached to the loaded wagon with a number of young rebels following, running as fast as booze and fear would allow, trying to catch the wagon.

After the dust settled, one of the Yankee soldiers was pointing up the road. There was the old Irishman, kneeling over a body lying in the road. At first, I was confused, but then it became clear that Olivia had followed us out of the house and when the shooting started, she started running towards us. One of the wild shots must have hit her.

I do not know where the Irishmen came from, but apparently quite close because he was already hovering over her. Even over the distance we could hear him sobbing, crying and howling, "Jesus Christ, those damn fools, they shot my daughter, oh lord forgive me for I am only just a damn foolish mortal, please bring back my daughter, I'll do anything, take this old fool's life instead." He quit sobbing and crying and fell over her body as if to protect her, to prevent God or man from harming her.

Jeffery, the local Yankee soldier, touched him on the shoulder and said, "We are all pilgrims. Her journey was completed." Turning to us, he said, "We need to get our butts out of here before they regroup.

Before we took off, I wanted to see for myself, and I checked for a pulse. She was only unconscious, with a slight head wound. I looked at the Irish man and said, "She will be okay. Just take care of her."

So, I, Theodore Washington Jones, the educated negro, was now part of the army defeating the confederacy. The Portsmouth Militia was rolled into the Major General Mc Pherson 4568 infantry and I was officially now part of the Union Army, (July 17, 1862, the US Congress passed two statutes allowing for the enlistment of 'colored' troops) had made it official, Black Americans can serve, while not quite equal to their white American, (half pay) we were now officially fighting for our freedom after a couple of hundred years fighting unofficially. As a black field first sergeant, black officers, not allowed at that time, I served as Captain Ludwick's agilent. I serve in that capacity through the Atlantic Campaign and the march to the sea Campaign. The end was clearly in sight, and I decided it was time for me to move on. The rest of the Union Army could finish the job of defeating the Rebels.

I was heading for California to invest my $1000, the money from the sale of my Ohio property, in California land. With Captain Ludwick's approval, I was mustard out of the army, board a Yankee clipper in Savannah, heading for San Francisco. Aboard, I met a San Francisco businessman who had invested with a Horner brother's land developer and had done well. He recommended them and offered to introduce me as Theodore Washington Jones, Southern Black Man land investor. I was going north. I did not want to be labeled a Southern Black Man investor, so I insisted on a land investor, TW Jones.

At first the businessmen were reluctant to do business with a black man but when they realized I was well educated—I wish, no, it was the $1000 in cash that made the difference—they decided they could do business with a black man, and they proved to be useful. Along with providing investment opportunities, they provided financial connections. One of these connections, Mr. Pioche, had acquired a large section of the Rancho San Miguel and was looking to sell a portion of it. It seemed the property had an issue, a fraudulent gold mine scam associated with it. He wanted to distance himself from it.

You know, it seemed to be destiny; I sold an acre with the mine and a cabin, a cabin built by that slave pirate Lynch, to a woman clerk, the negro seamstress from Logan's corner, Olivia, she is going under Mary Kelly but I recognized her right away, I only met her one time but she was unforgettable, not sure why but I had the same feeling, a desire to be with her.

TW Jones stood up, without any to-do, and said, "Well, Bryan, I've bored you sufficiently, sure you've got places to see and things to do, I'll be on my way, don't overdo the Jamison, be careful, perhaps we will meet again in some cycle."

So, there I sat, Bryan, in a high-back chair, the smoke of Arturo Fuente Hemingway cigar curling above a glass of Jamison, Johnny Ace's *Pledging My Love*, still playing, the sailors comparing bar tales as if no time had passed, no TW Jones, yet TW Jones's exploits were still ringing in my ears. I am still amazed by the whole episode. But this was not the last of T W Jones.

A few years later I was in New Orleans for a holiday , a short holiday, I needed to keep a New Orleans visits short but sweet, too much carousing. I like to wander about, no itinerary or plan, just checking out somewhere new. Savannah and New Orleans are great cities to wander about, but my favorite is New Orleans and particularly the French Quarter with its narrow alleys, antique shops, and off-the-beaten-path bars. To me, they embraced the history and beauty of the past. I'm not talking about Bourbon St, the main raise-hell street. The best wandering is off Bourbon, quieter streets like, Royal, Dauphine, St Peter, they retains the elegance of the past.

So, a number of years ago, April 2, 1990s, somewhat in my prime— well, I thought so, anyway—I was returning from a rather enjoyable night of music, drinks and so on. I was heading to my night logging on Burgundy Street, but first, I thought of stopping by The Port of Call, a bar on N Rampart, great hamburger, baked potato, fixings. On the way there, I passed Lafitte's, one of the oldest, and I must say my favorite bar. I decided to stop there and have one more for the road.

I left the bar with adequate liquor under my belt but quite in control, physically and mentally, and as I turned the corner onto Bienville St, I noticed an elegant roll of shotgun bungalows 100 feet or so on the right. Now, I had been there on the street many times but had not observed them before. They were handsome, almost looked freshly built. As I remembered, there had been an ugly commercial structure there. Sitting on the steps of the middle unit, I noticed a man. He seemed to be looking in my direction. The Quarters is relatively safe; it is kind of the golden goose for the city and the word on the street is do your crime anywhere but not in the Quarters.

Nonetheless, I started to cross the street to avoid confronting this man. I thought he might be associated with those young colored girls I met in a bar, and I had been marked, an easy mark. I had just started to step off the curb when he stood up, looking down the street past me. He turned to pick up some luggage, a rather handsome carpet bag, and a cane. I had that feeling of déjà vu; I felt I had met him before but could not recall where.

I could hear an approaching carriage and horses on the stone pavement. The carriage passed by me and stopped in front of the bungalow where he was now standing. As he walked down the steps, he dropped the cane; it tumbled down the steps, bounced a couple of times and stopped directly in front of me. I picked it up and noted how elaborate it was. It had the Army of Mississippi carved in bold letters and a silver cap. I handed it to him. He looked at it, examined me for a moment and asked, "Have we met, I believe we have but cannot quite recall? Young man, what is your name?"

Well, I liked being called a young man at my age, but I was still concerned. I took a step backward, looked and noticed the street was lit by gaslights and the street was paved with red bricks with the residue of horse manure.

Okay, I thought, *maybe I am not holding my liquor. This is really getting strange.*

This man was now standing a few feet away and I could see by gaslight that he was well dressed but old-fashioned, a three-piece suit, vest, and gold chain and all. He was a large man, European features with African blood. He said, "Do not be concerned," and he extended his arm for a handshake.

At this point, I had a decision to make, turn and run or accept his handshake. But I had a feeling, think I knew this man, hell I am sure but it had been awhile, in a past cycle. Well, I decided what the hell, why not, let's see where it goes.

"By your dress, I believe you are a Westerner. Perhaps you have been to California. I lived in San Francisco back in the 1870s. I was in real estate and did well. How about you, young man?" he said as he looked me over.

I thought he said, 'In the 1870s', no, Did he mean the 1970s?

"Well, sir, I am an engineer by trade, but my real love is wandering around. I'm Bryan," and held out my hand.

We shook hands, and he replied, "I know I met you a few years ago in your life cycle."

Theodore Washington Jones, I thought, *wow this cannot be true;* "Theodore Washington Jones?" I replied and looked to see his reaction.

"Yes, do you prefer Bryan or Johnny?" he asked, and without waiting for an answer he said, "We met before, do you remember that mining town in California, you were wearing a garbage bag for rain paraphernalia? And then at a dive in San Francisco you were smoking a cigar? This time, we are in my cycle but come sit on the porch and I'll tell you the story about becoming a landowner," he said as he motioned towards the steps and as I sat down he began his tail.

"Bryan, after the war and the confederacy were beaten, I headed west to seek my fortune there. The transcontinental railroad was completed and only a few days' travel to the Pacific coast and people were streaming into San Francisco, the real estate market was booming. I took a Yankee Clipper, Savannah to San Francisco, I fell in love with San Francisco, great city and even greater investment. There were a number of real estate associations investing in land. I acquired a large section of land in the old Rancho San Miguel; it had been in foreclosure, and I purchase it from Mr. Pioche, real bargain. I subdivided it and sold off most of it, but retained an acre or so with a cabin. I sold it to a young lady, Olivia. She had changed her name, was going by the name Mary and considered white by all the locals. But to me, she was still Olivia and beautiful black or white. Funny how small the world is. She was a slave girl, a tailor, that made my suit in Logan's Corner. I believe the Lieutenant told you the story about how the rebels tried to capture me there."

"Yes, I remember. How could I forget, but I thought it had to be a dream or something, not for real? I was hitchhiking years ago, and the Lieutenant gave me a ride. But what is this cycle stuff?" I asked.

Theodore looked away, then looked at me and said, "That is another story, perhaps sometime in the future, but for now, I am going to tell you my version of a love story, you see. I believe Olivia and I are destined to meet and be lovers."

"That's quite a story, Theodore," I said, "but what does it have to do with me?"

"Well, Bryan, or John, you are a special person," he said, "and I do not know why but we seem to cross cycle periodically, perhaps there is a reason but maybe it's just chaos, but perhaps it is because you are a storyteller. So now I need to be on my way, and you need to return to your night lodging and in the morning, this might just be another dream, one you are not sure you dreamed or not. Till we meet again, I bid you *adieu*."

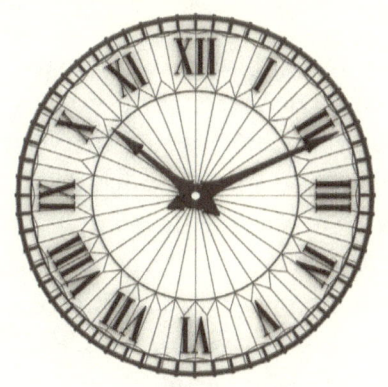

Chapter 14

MARY KELLY

Becoming a Free American Woman

The clouds, dark and threatening to unleash their rain, water accumulated from the Pacific Ocean, blown eastward by the wind, now hovering over the canyon. The black top road, Bosworth Street, ends and turns into a narrow dirt road as it enters the park, my favorite access to the park. The dirt road winds its way through a row of large blue gum eucalyptus trees, past the area where the Islais creek is diverted underground, the last of the free running water. From here, you can, if you choose, to follow the creek as it meanders through a few miles of willow trees. The Y of its branches made fine sling shots, real important in my youth. Once, this section of the creek was much larger with a watershed of the surrounding Glen Canyon, but the encroachment of residential development greatly reduced the watershed, and the creek of my youth is long gone, and its place is little more than a trickle. It is still a creek, and I still enjoy tracking it up to its end. But this day, I had a goal, to meet Olivia, I do not know how or why, but I had a strong feeling that she would be there somewhere.

About a quarter of a mile up the creek on the left side there is a slide area created by the building of O'Shaughnessy Blvd., 1935 W.P.A project, the creek makes a hard right turn and widens there before narrowing again as it works its way up through the canyon. Back in the days of my youth, it was the only deep section. It was my favorite spot. Water bugs populated this section, and I would marvel at their ability to zip across the pond. I anticipated a pretty much dried out section there as I rounded the turn but to my surprise the pond was still there, bigger than ever, no rockslide, nestled between a steep incline covered in dried gold-colored wide oats with outcrops of reddish colored sedimentary rock here and there and lined with green willow trees. The whole scene seemed to switch to another time, another place, and there was Olivia, older but still with traces of youth. I said, "Hello, Olivia. Somehow, I knew I would see you today, there something about the canyon that makes me think of you."

"Mary, I am no longer Olivia. I've been Mary for a number of years now. Johnny, is that your name? she asked.

Replying, I said, "It is Bryan, but I was once Johnny, just as you were once Olivia and now you are Mary. But I must ask you, how did I get here? Clearly, this is not my time, everything here is not as it was? And I must ask, is this real, do you and I really exist?"

Without answering those questions, she replied, "Yes and no, but I do not know or care. What I do know is you are here, I am here, and this is a beautiful place, creek, and time we are sharing. Bryan, oh you've grown old, you see your cycle has a different time rate. But do not worry, I am here only to continue my story.

"James, my almost father, had a brother, Mr. M Kelly, in San Francisco and after the near miss, all most got killed, a stray Rebel bullet, at Logan's Corner, James decided it was time to set me free and get out of the south. Mr. M Kelly's hardware store was doing well, and he could use some help, so James decided to send me there."

It took almost two months to travel from New Orleans to San Francisco. I'd been seasick most of it but as the steamship approach San Francisco Bay, I had an elevating feeling of freedom, a new year, a new world, free of being confined to the shipboard, free of the social and class confines of the South and free to be myself in a new world.

I will never forget how beautiful San Francisco Bay looked that morning. The entrance was shrouded in fog and as the ship pierced through it, the bay opened to a vast body of water, surrounded by gentle slopes of golden-brown hills. I felt as if a whole new world awaited me.

The steam ship, Columbus from Panama, docked at P Mial's pier, January 2, 1863, an hour late. I was excited, nervous, and scared. I'd never been this far from home and all alone.

A man, I think one of the crew said, "Young lady, you should go to the office over there." He pointed. "There is someone waiting. I believe a Mr. Kelly is here to get a shipment and meet a lady. I believe that's you."

I was uneasy, apprehensive, and felt lost. A man approached and asked, "Mary?"

I turned and looked at him, replied, "Yes, sir," in my best white man's English. He seemed surprised by my appearance. I guess he did not expect me to be as attractive. I was listed as a white woman, Mary Kelly, en route to meet her uncle Michael Kelly. Jame Kelly knew if he listed me as Olivia, a negro, I'd have to travel third class, as a white woman he could secure a second-class passage. Clearly my African blood showed through my appearance, but then I was in California , a new state with a blend of many nationalities, Italian, Spanish, Chinese, and what all, was just white enough I guess to be accepted as white.

I was determined to be a free American woman, black or white, and felt all that stuff about blood was nothing more than an excuse to enslave people. I know there is an advantage in the way people treated you when you are considered white, so I played along. It is not that I was ashamed of my African blood; I understood how strong, courageous, and brave my African ancestors must have been to survive, but I also had European ancestors equally strong and besides, there's no harm in it.

Mr. M Kelly picked up my luggage, loaded on his buckboard with his hardware and said, "Well, young lady, I hope you enjoy San Francisco."

He helped me up on the wagon and asked me to please hold the hardware invoices to prevent being lost. The 'please' part of the request almost overwhelmed me. It felt great to be asked with a 'please', as an equal.

I took the invoices, looked him in the eyes and with a slight Irish hint to southern accent, after all I'd spent most of my life in an Irish household, said, "My pleasure, sir."

Mr. M Kelly, retaining the eye contact, replied, "Mr. Kelly or Michael, but not sir, lass the Irish do not like the uppity sir, a bit like royalty."

On the long ride from the dock, Mr. Kelly talked about this hardware store and the area's history. He said it was located in the San Miguel Hills area, locally called Glen Park now, part of the old Rancho San Miguel and was connected to the city via the old missionary road and it was still the main route to the waterfront.

He took the waterfront road, Embarcadero, he said. It was very busy, with wharfs, docked ships with tall mask, flat steam ships with no masks, all very busy, men of all types and nationalities scurrying about. He turned south on a road he said was the old missionary route to San Miguel Hills. I was impressed by how much construction was going on and how disconnected they seemed to be. Portions were quite new with three- and four-story buildings, Victorian style, Mr. Kelly said, and other one-story abodes Spanish style. I remember Mr. Kelly pointed out a section dominated with adobe structures and the original mission, Mission Dolores, almost in total ruins. I had a feeling of loss when I thought how it once was alive with activity and hope and now just an old, abandoned mission, forsaken, alone but as we neared his store, I was delighted by the activity, the life ,the beauty of the free running creek that flows under the Diamond Street bridge next to Mr. Kelly's hardware store.

Mr. Kelly seemed impressed by my reading of the invoices. I checked the numbers to be sure the addition was correct. Mr. Kelly said, "I think you will be good at accounting tasks. You could work with the customer and when time permits, do some of the accounting work."

I was a young, attractive woman in the west, which was mostly populated by men. And so, I drew a lot of attention, which I skillfully handled. But one male kept staring at me as if he recognized me. Mr. Kelly said he thought he was from the south and perhaps an ex- confederate soldier.

Just the word 'confederate' created a feeling of fear and dread, but his posture was more friendly. Then one day he asked, "Are you from Logan's Corner? Did you work in a tailor's shop?"

I was surprised. Logan's Corner was a small, unimportant town in Kentucky. *How could he know?* I thought but did not answer.

He said without waiting, "You worked in a tailor's shop, you made a uniform for me. Do you remember?" and without waiting he said, "I remember you, Olivia," and held out his hand, "I am Tom Lynch."

I looked at this hand for a moment and replied as Mary Kelly, "I believe you are mistaken, sir, can I help you?"

He smiled and with a knowing look and his hand still extended, said, "Pardon me, Mary."

I accepted his handshake and said, "Can I help you?" in a business-like tone and a slight Irish accent.

Oh Bryan, I remember that feeling of freedom as I headed out for a Sunday soul journey. While others attended church for the salvation of their souls, I would tracked up Islais Creek into Glen Canyon. It was March, the creek running full and free, the golden dry wild oats giving way to the green of the new generation, sprinkling of bright yellow wildflowers, the next generation of California poppies, and-here-and-there the purple of the Douglas iris dotted the canyon slopes. Red-tailed hawks soaring and ground squirrels scurrying for shelter, the eternal struggle of life. The whole spectrum was a delight to my eyes and senses, renewed my appreciation for life.

There was already talk about covering the creek to enhance the developing business area, but to me, the wild free flow of it brought pleasure to my heart, kind of like my release from slavery and life in the South. It was my second trip this month. I found an abandoned cabin in the hills above the canyon. People said it had been a miner's cabin. I loved the open free feeling of the area. I knew in my heart that, if possible, I wanted to buy the cabin, fix it up and live in it. It excited me to imagine that I could own the cabin, just mine, and even if it was just a cabin, it would be my home.

On my way home from the soul journey, my path went through the glen meadow where the creek exited the canyon. It was getting late in the morning, but still had the morning feeling. I noticed a group of people near the edge of the meadow, near the trees, having a picnic. It seemed odd, too early. Perhaps they were downtown people, out for the day, and just started a bit early. As I approached them, I realized they were not picnickers, rather they appeared to be camping, being there overnight.

A man standing, pointed at me and said, "*Gringo*," and then something in Spanish, and they all started laughing. I did not understand Spanish, but I recognized the belligerent warring in it.

Another man stood up and with a Mexican accent in English said, "You southern gringos are slow in the head. Do you know today is the Sabbath? You should be in church, not wandering around disturbing the poor. Aren't satisfied stealing our land now you want to disrupt our peace? Go back to your country, and your own black slaves, stole our land, now you enslave *pobre hombre*.

A third man said, "You must excuse my *amigo*. He is upset but doesn't mean any harm," then he turned to the other man and said something in Spanish.

I could pick up a few English words: hardware, lady, and work. I then recognized the man as a customer and handyman who works for Mr. M. Kelly. I did not want to antagonize them, so I proceeded on my way, but it was a lesson. You know Johnny, I realized prejudice is not exclusively black and white. The more I thought about it, I realized everyone is capable of being prejudiced, including myself. Every day at work, women gossip about a neighbor whose kids are running around with the Chins. A man saying, "They're Mexican, they'll steal from you". Clearly, there is prejudice against blacks, not to the extent of the south but still prevalent. And now, being Mary, a white woman, I was considered one of those gringos, the people that had stolen, pilfered their land.

Interrupting her story I said, Mary, I am Bryan, Johnny was the young boy I was, I am now Bryan.

Alright you are Bryan now but the first time I met you, you a still a wet behind the ears boy, remember that woman in that shiny black auto that roll down the window asked you if you were one of those immigrant that moved into the cabin? With out waiting for an answer she proceeded with her story:

I, Mary, was grateful that I was considered a white woman, but now I realized being white does not shield or make me immune to prejudice, discrimination, bigotry. Yet I felt a little guilty as I recognized how

112

my African ancestors had suffered and sacrificed to survive, and how unbearable my mother's pain must have been being in love and loved by someone but not being able to acknowledge it. To me, the whiteness stuff was part of my freedom, one less bondage, one less obstacle to being free. I rationalized that was in the past, my life is in the future and in those days, being identified as white is the smart thing.

Interrupting her story, I asked, Mary, that was you in the auto?

One of Mr. Kelly's customers, she continued without addressing my question, was complaining about a cabin up in the hill that belonged to Mr. TW Jones, and he needed to kick out vagrants who used the cabin regularly. Mr. M Kelly knew the cabin. It had been part of a gold mine stock scam. The customer indicated that Mr. TW Jones wanted to sell it and if he was interested or knew of someone interested to contact him; he was the foreman for Mr. TW Jones and was authorized to sell it. Mr. M Kelly remembered me saying how I loved the area and thought the cabin might be used as a dwelling. Up to this point, I had been living in the small shed in the rear of his property, Mr. M Kelly, always a businessman, saw an opportunity to purchase a section of land about the cabin and sell a portion with the cabin to me, on credit to be worked off on overtime.

With the completion of the railroad, many Chinese were looking for work. I employed a few to make additions to the cabin, a second story, a lean-to as a bedroom, a back porch. I was impressed with their skill; I was told they could only do rough work, digging tunnels, laying tracks, but the Chinese were quite good carpenters. For the first time in my life, a property owner, a person of means, not much but mine. I could not help but to think how my life has changed, from an adopted slave to a free white businesswoman, a property owner.

Mr. M Kelly, the businessman, opportunist, suggested that he and I might open an upscale Tailor's Shop in San Francisco. With the gold country money pouring into the city, tailored suits along with tall hats were in high demand. My tailoring skills and Mr. M Kelly's business brain made a great partnership.

A major obstacle was the cabin. I was reluctant to move; I was quite happy living there in the undeveloped hills above the Glen Canyon, but I was a smart young woman and could see it offered a real opportunity. It was difficult to travel downtown. I decided to rent a space in the newly constructed building down the street from the hardware store and improve the cabin. It turns out that TW Jones was my new landlord.

As Mary, I had plenty of suitors, a few were serious, but I so relish my new status—free landowner. But there was another secret suitor who had flowers delivered to my newly purchased cabin. The card was handwritten:

'Mary, Olivia; I need to thank you for saving my life and the wonderful, tailored suit. TW Jones.'

I thought or maybe hoped it was Theodore Washington Jones but could not believe it could be, once the educated negro farmer, now a land investor, businessman, and here in San Francisco but it must be, he knew I was once Olivia, a slave.

But now, I had a major issue with my new freedom.

I believed TW Jones would ask me to be his wife. I could love him, but I was reluctant to give up my life as a self-sufficient, independent white woman. To be a mixed couple, black and white, was unheard of and really frowned upon. Then there were the children, they could show their African roots, have to face all that prejudice stuff. I had decided not to accept his proposal and continue with my own dream.

We agreed to meet for lunch that afternoon; I felt he would expect an answer. The day seemed to just be dragging on, few customers, a terrible feeling I might be making a mistake.

I prepared lunch at home and brought it to the shop. I preferred home cooking to bought food. Just as I finished setting up the table, a young woman of color entered and said, "Can I have a moment of your time?" She seemed so familiar, like she had always known me. In a soft southern accent with clearly an African touch, she said, "Afua, using my African name, a name my mother gave me. The agony, pain of losing your independence, enduring racism is nothing compared to the pain, regret of losing your chance to live, love, share a life with one so special. I know because I had to endure both, but had no choice." She turned, proceeded to leave with one last look over her shoulder, a mother to her child look, and was gone.

So now Bryan, Mary was in a real fix. I was a now a businesswoman, the landowner, facing a major dilemma: three suitors.

Mr. Lynch, the ex-confederate officer, white and prosperous even with his history he was an attractive man. I rationalized people make mistakes, he only did what many people in the south were doing, but never harmed me, never divulged my secret, allowing me to continue my image as a white woman and always treated me with respect, even when I was a slave. He just purchased a fine Edwardian on Broadway in Pacific Heights, said it needs a mistress and wants me to marry him and live there with him. If I accepted his offer, I could live in the community as a respected upper-class lady. But Bryan, I thought, a bird in a gilded cage, a trophy. Not freedom.

Mr. TW Jones, that beautiful black man I tailored a suit for back in Logan's Corner, was courting me. TW Jones, a successful, respected entrepreneur, was planning to return to farming, He'd purchased a large section of land in the San Joaquin Valley and asked me to be his wife and move with him to the valley. He plans to build a plantation-like empire there, including building a large Victorian-style farmhouse, grow crops, raise animals and have many children. But Bryan, a bird in a gilded cage, devoted loved wife, busy mother, not freedom.

Mary, my alter ego, the ex slave, the independent American woman free from the color barrier, the businesswoman with a successful tailoring business, she had sufficient income to support my lifestyle, to update my new cabin, to enjoy my freedom, to do as I damn well pleased. No man to answer to, no children to care for——freedom.

Bryan this was my choice, freedom. But I paid for it dearly, the pain, and regret for losing my chance to live, love, share a life with someone. It is strange how fate can repeat itself, slavery, prevented my mother from a life with the man she loved, and the need for freedom prevented me from sharing my life with the one I could have loved, Theodore Washington Jones.

Dumfounded, here I am Bryan, once Johnny the want-to-be -someone, listening to a story, a tail of long ago, told by a onetime slave, now Mary, a independent free American woman, I met in my youth, when I was Johnny and she was Olivia, by a fire, not far from where I am standing by this creek in Glen Canyon in another tine, not my time cycle , I guess her time cycle, without a clue, how can this be and so must ask Mary, why, how is this for real?

With out my asking and how she knew I have no idea, but she said, cycle are things that have a beginning, and a end but they do not have to stop. For what ever reason our cycles have a common cross over point, period of commingle , possibly the mine cabin is the key but be that as it may I have always and will always known you, Johnny , Bryan , so ours it not to know why but to believe.

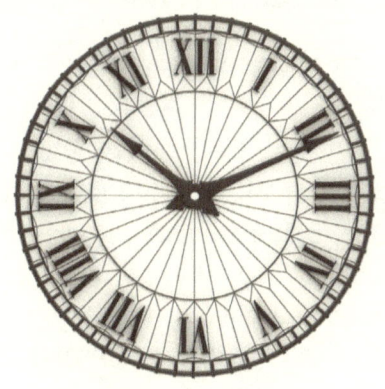

Chapter 15

Changes

Return to Cabin Site

Change, the only thing you can count on. Cycles by definition require changes, from a beginning to an end. I am, we are, everything is in a cycle, at least that I know of. Therefore I, you, we exist in many different cycles. Clearly cycles can intersect, commingle, after all how else could a species like homo sapiens propagate through time. I think all cycle with time as a parameter mingle periodically and often exchange material be it element, component, energy. Our rocky planet, earth is definitely in a cycle, a cycle generated by who knows what, resulting in molten magna movements forming, moving, creating, distorting continents, forming the terrain we live on. It seems to me this terrain has an artistic character to it, not just random stuff but stuff that's beautiful, interesting, threatening. The earth's terrain change is in a rather large cycle, the hills of San Francisco are only a minute portion of these changes and change to old San Miguel Noe's terrain is even a smaller portion but to my in a minuscule life cycle the changes were enormous.

Changes are everywhere, in everything, all the time and in my cycle the people I've known, places I've been, person I've been, an illiterate schoolboy, a clueless teenager, a US Navy sailor, a Silicon Valley engineer, a dirt bike rider searching for freedom, a family man doing the best I can, and now, an old man propagating yarns and even though you might be skeptical or just bored, disappointed about some of my ventures, I only hope they were entertaining, brought you pleasure.

Gone with the winds of Change, 444 Sussex is long gone, no trace of the cabin, gold mine, only paved streets and houses. With the help of earth-moving equipment, the hills of Rancho San Miguel have been transformed into Diamond Heights, an upscale residential neighborhood. But the memories still exist, the Saturday mornings, no school, grass still damp from the morning fog, creek running clear, wonderful wide open thousand acres of the old Rancho Miguel to explore—freedom, freedom, freedom.

Freedom to share with Cindy, Oh you don't know Cindy. It seem like forever ago but it was only eighty odd years ago I shared a life cycle with a little black female terrier, Cindy. We, my brother and I, recent immigrants to the park, Glen Park, just two boys, exploring our new world. At the end of Bosworth Street, where the black top ends and the dirt road lined with giant eucalyptus trees we met a very young Scottie Terrier. Perhaps she was lost or may be strayed a bit from her home but in any case we declared her lost and in need of a new home. We picked her up and hurried to 444 Sussex and introduced her to Mom. Well Mom was less than excited but being Mom with loads of compassion and knowledge welcomed her to our home. Well I guess because I was the youngest or maybe not old enough to know better she became my dog. I cared for, well you know, I took care of her and she returned it with the pure love, total devotion. For the next few years we, my dog and I roamed the hills, the creeks, the valleys that were once José de Jesús's Noé domain, Rancho San Miguel, a gift of the nearly defunct Mexican Government. But then Cindy matured faster then I and developed a relationship with a handsome Beagle Terrier, King, who lived in the neighborhood. Well I had my struggles the San Francisco Education system, Cindy had her's raising adorable mongrel Beagle Terriers. Ok, I did make a little money selling them but it was not easy to part from them but it was easy to love them. Well the problems with cycles are they have endings and some are longer then other but natural endings are one thing abrupt are another. Don't want to dwell on the details but I was on my way to the navy and her's to the pound, no one to care for her, she was just an old dog but there was one last look, as she was being loaded on to the San Francisco Animal Control Wagon she looked at me with an acknowledgment and farewell. Well it seems most everything else has changed but that look, to this day I still see it, remember it, feel the pain, the pain has changed but little.

Parked on Diamond Heights Boulevard overlooking Glen Canyon, I think how much it has changed since I was a boy. A boulevard was a dirt road, the remains of the Rancho San Miguel. Gone are the narrow dirt roads, soaring red-tailed hawks, scampering ground squirrels, most of the wild oats, and in their place are paved roads, sidewalks, and houses. I can't help but wonder about all the changes I've witnessed over the past eighty plus years, all the technical progress, memories of my days, years in Silicon Valley, the struggles between a desire to live a free unscheduled life and be part of a highly organized, disciplined technical team. And all in the background of time, simply slipping away. Knowing it doesn't make a damn, it is what it is, and you are here on a one-way ticket, a cycle with a beginning and a end . That no matter what, you will be disappointed about some of your ventures and only hope that some are acceptable.

Is there any validity to lieutenant Ludwick's remarks " "The answer is clear. You can see it in every day and in every venue. Everything is a cycle, cycles in cycles, cycles with minuscule to infinite time periods. You cannot escape your cycle, but occasionally, you might get a glimpse into another."

Is my story possibly true, could my life cycle commingle with Olivera Afua Gilman, Theodore Washington Jones, and Azriell Thomas Lynch life cycles separated by hundreds of years. I know much of it is facts and maybe some of it is wishful thinking, a dreamers day dream. I apologize, just trash not even the gusto of Hemingway, not the class of Fitzgerald, not the poetic rhythm of Cohen, but a story, some truth, some fiction, some truth in the fiction but what the hell why not, maybe there is a zone or zones like the Twilight Zone with different set of rules, rather more interesting than this monadic zone commonly referred to as reality.

The Family 1958